The Odd 1s Out

Doodle Book

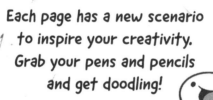

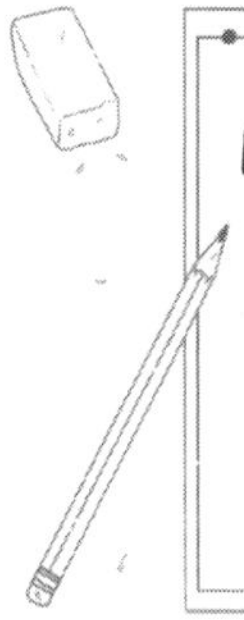

Each page has a new scenario
to inspire your creativity.
Grab your pens and pencils
and get doodling!

James Rallison

A TarcherPerigee I

D1468619

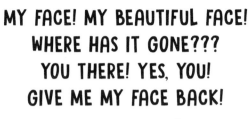

MY FACE! MY BEAUTIFUL FACE!
WHERE HAS IT GONE???
YOU THERE! YES, YOU!
GIVE ME MY FACE BACK!

Draw James a new face.

PHEW! WAIT . . . WHERE'S MY BODY? ACK! WHY DOES THIS KEEP HAPPENING TO ME? FIX ME, YOU DOODLING MASTER!

Draw James a new body.

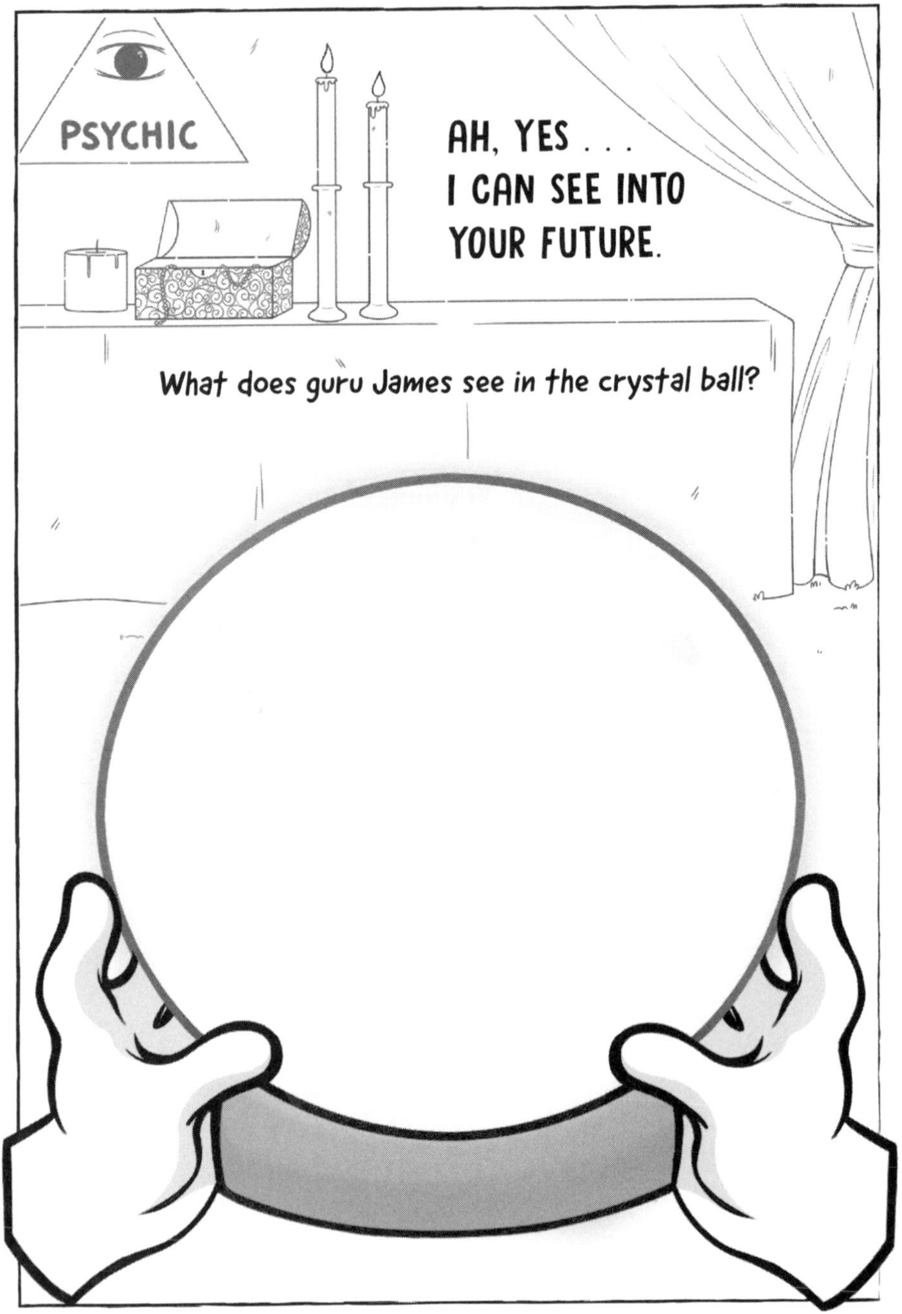
PSYCHIC
AH, YES . . .
I CAN SEE INTO
YOUR FUTURE.
What does guru James see in the crystal ball?

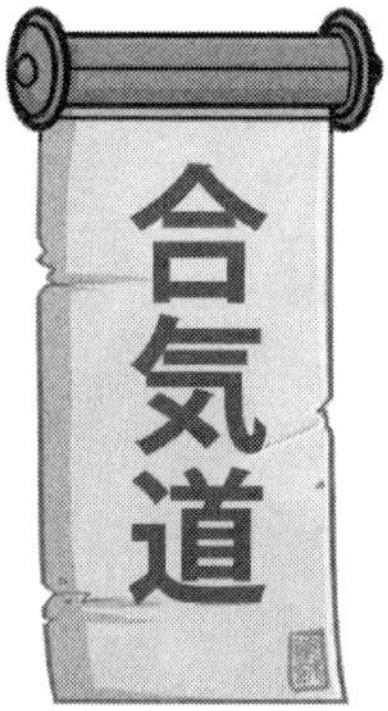
合気道

SHOW US SOME SWEET MOVES!

Draw yourself as a
martial arts black belt.

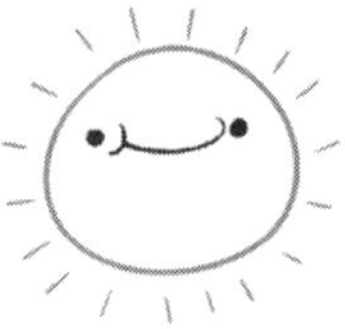

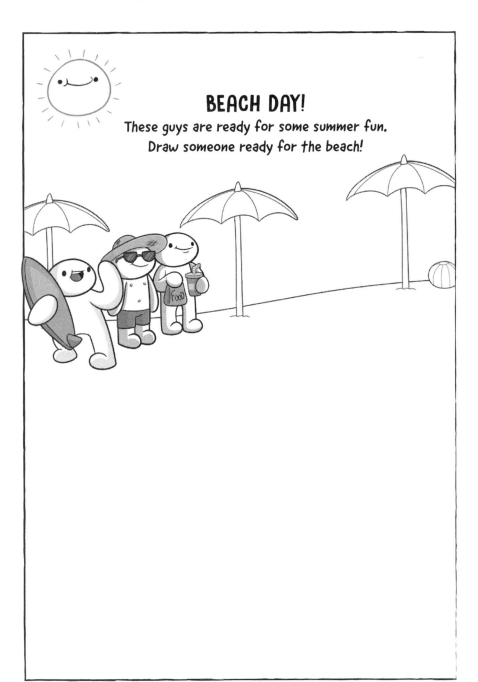

BEACH DAY!

These guys are ready for some summer fun.
Draw someone ready for the beach!

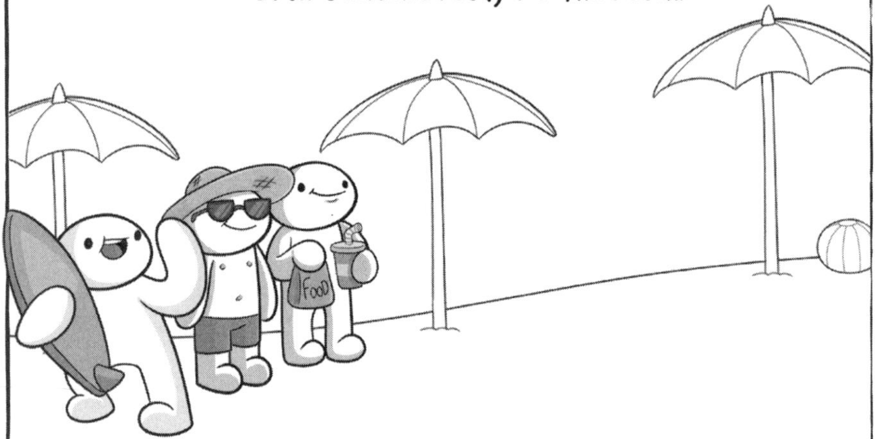
FOOD

DESIGN-A-CONE

An "everything" cone?
Uh, I don't know if we make those.
Why don't you make one yourself?

DJ TURN IT UP!

Draw yourself standing
behind the DJ booth.

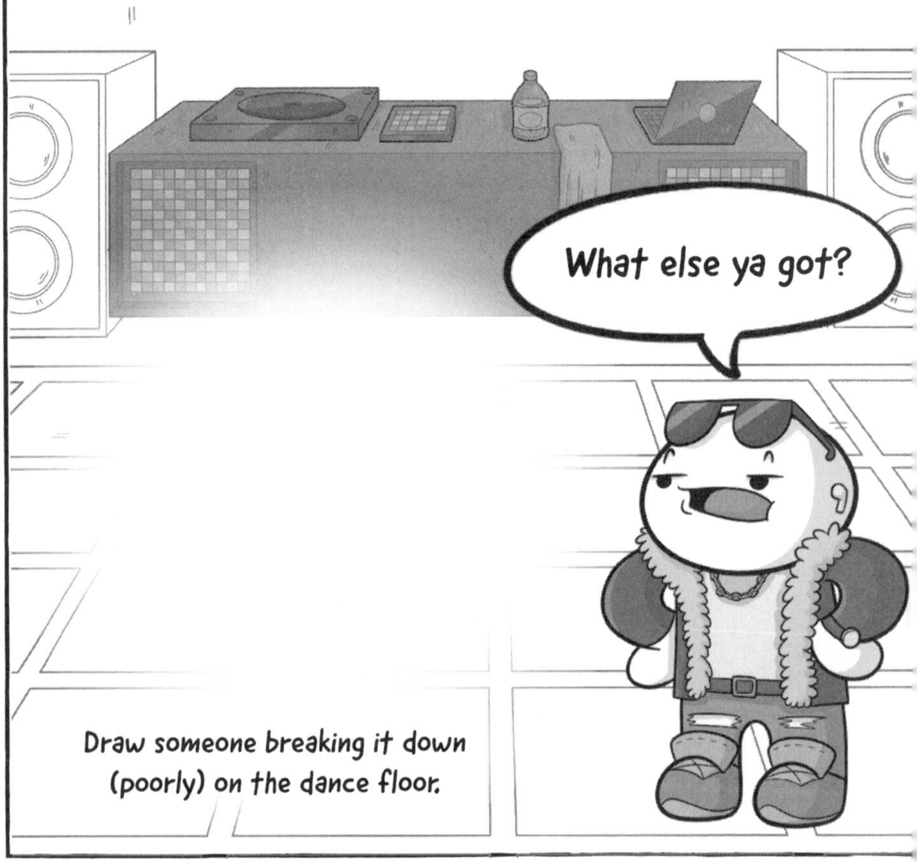
What else ya got?

Draw someone breaking it down
(poorly) on the dance floor.

IT'S A DANCE BATTLE!

Draw a dancer tearing it up
on the dance floor.

SAY CHEESE!

Draw your family portrait, or
maybe one of you and your
best friends!

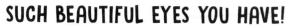

SUCH BEAUTIFUL EYES YOU HAVE!

All the better to doodle!

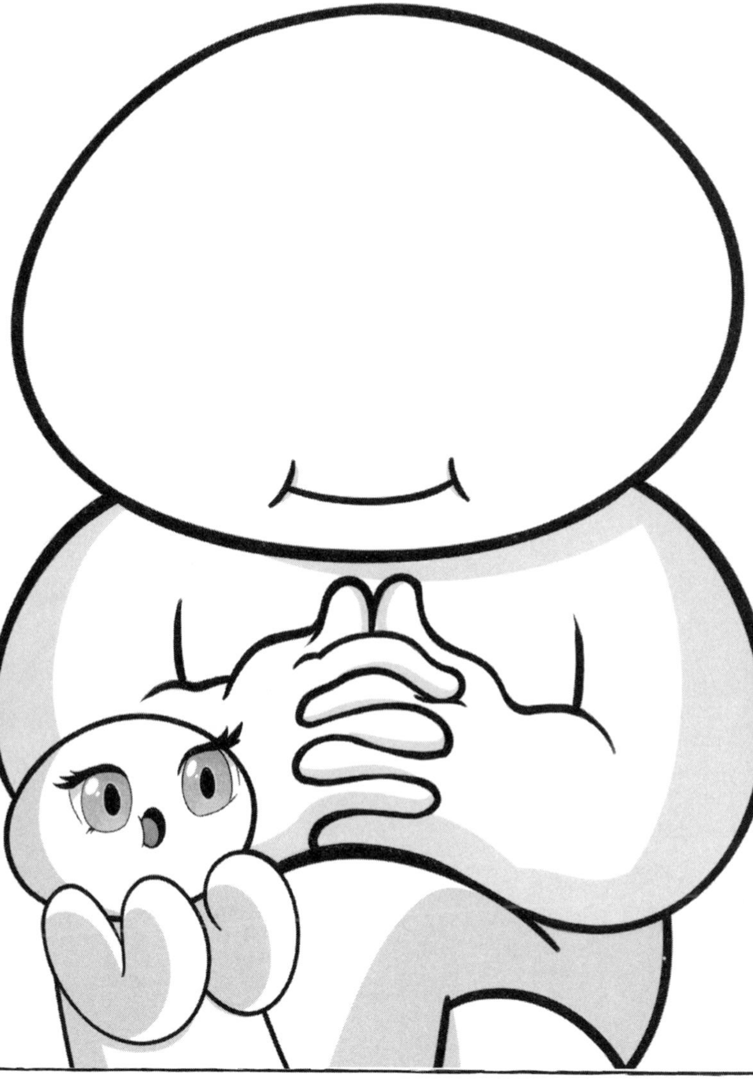

HEY! WHAT ARE YOU DOING IN THERE?!

What has snuck its way inside this kangaroo's pouch?

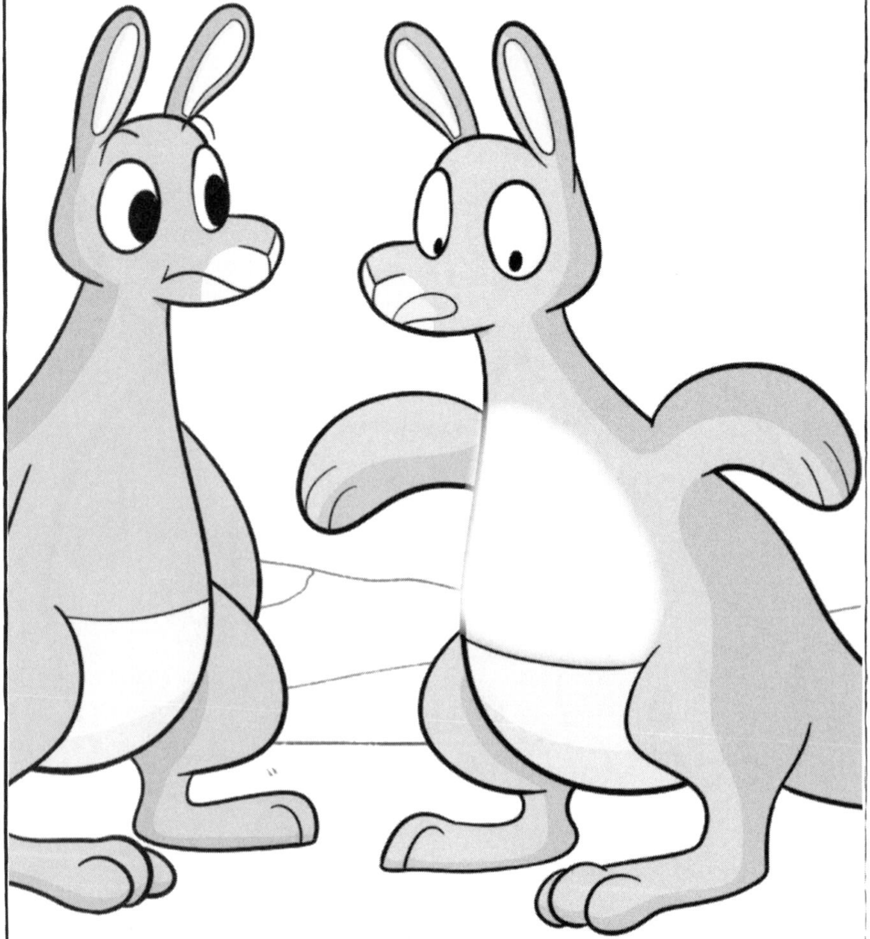

WHAT AM I LOOKING AT HERE, EXACTLY?

This lion-snake is pretty odd.
Try mixing up some other animal hybrids to be his friends!

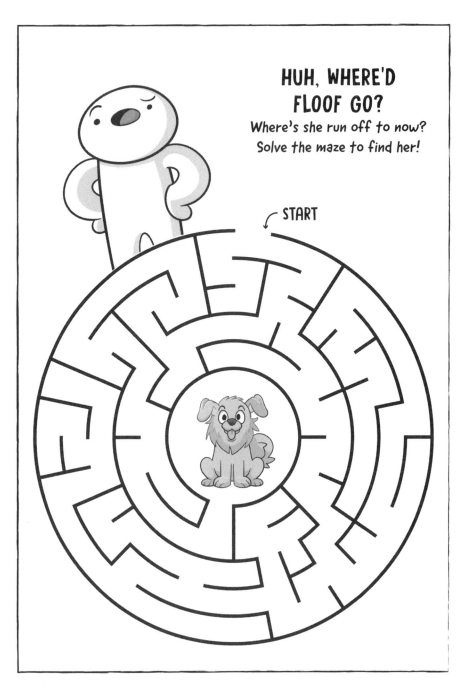

HUH, WHERE'D FLOOF GO?

Where's she run off to now?
Solve the maze to find her!

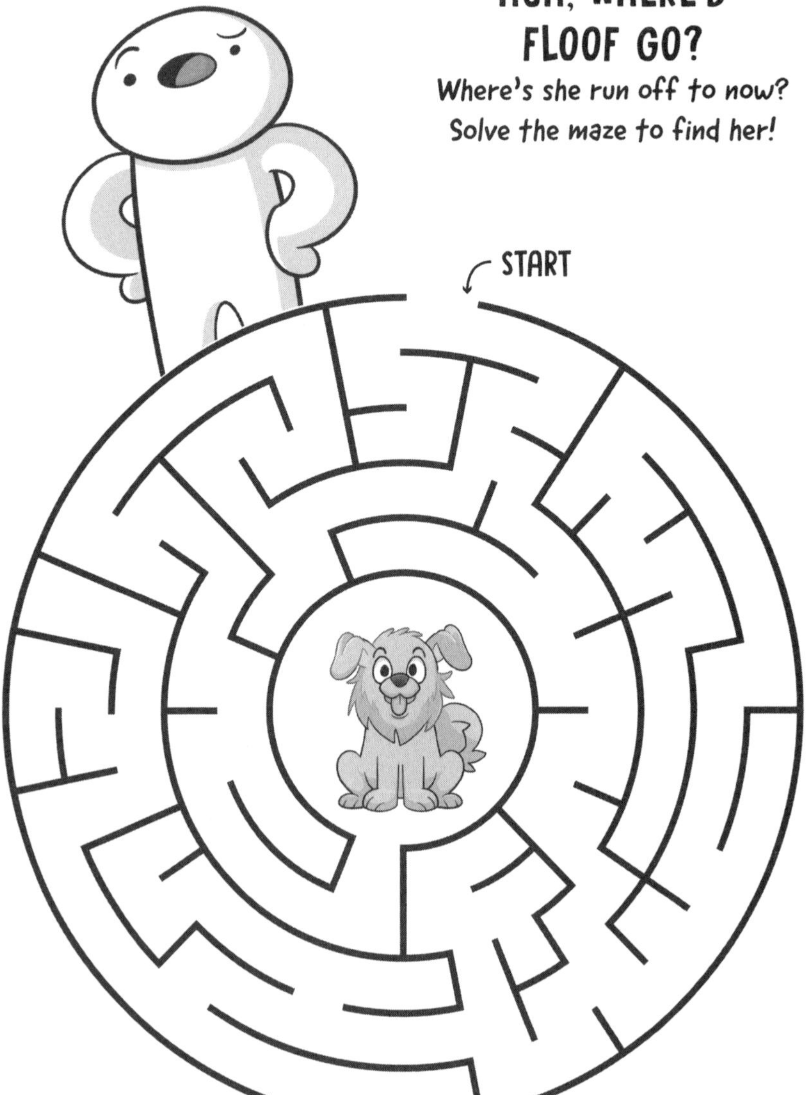
START

YOUR HIGHNESS, PLEASE . . . I DON'T THINK THAT'S APPROPRIATE ATTIRE FOR A RULER.

Well, who's in charge of the dress code here? You!
Design your royal outfit as you sit upon your throne.

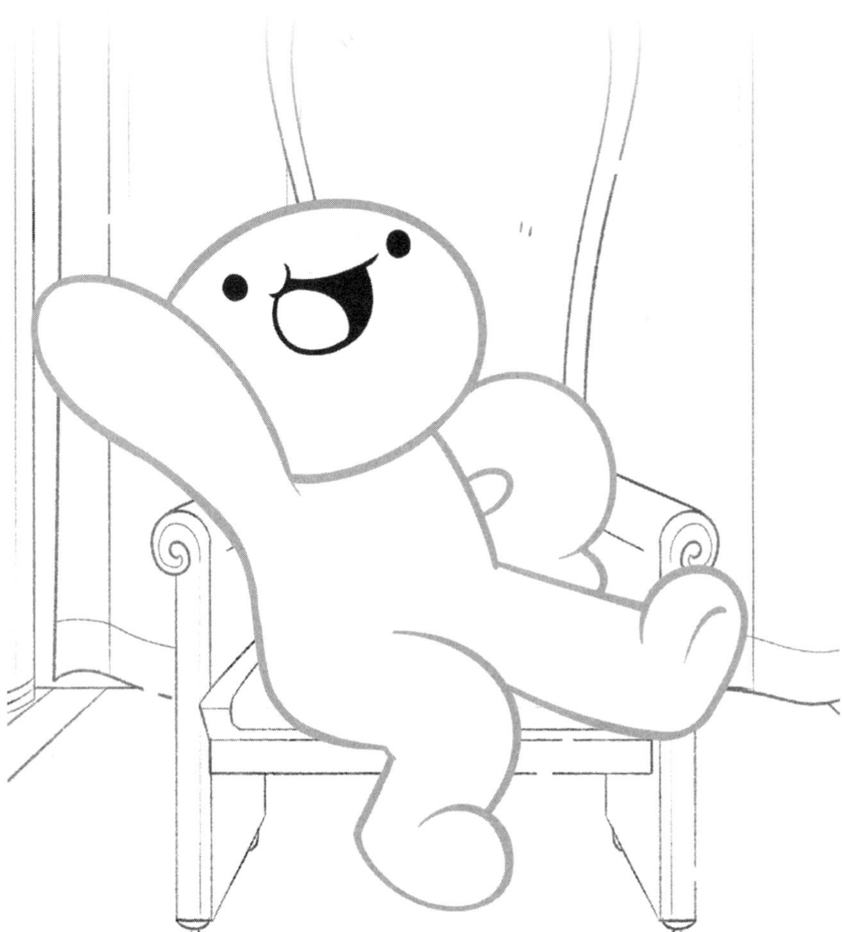

MONEY, MONEY, MONEY.

Might be funny . . . if you drew yourself on this money.

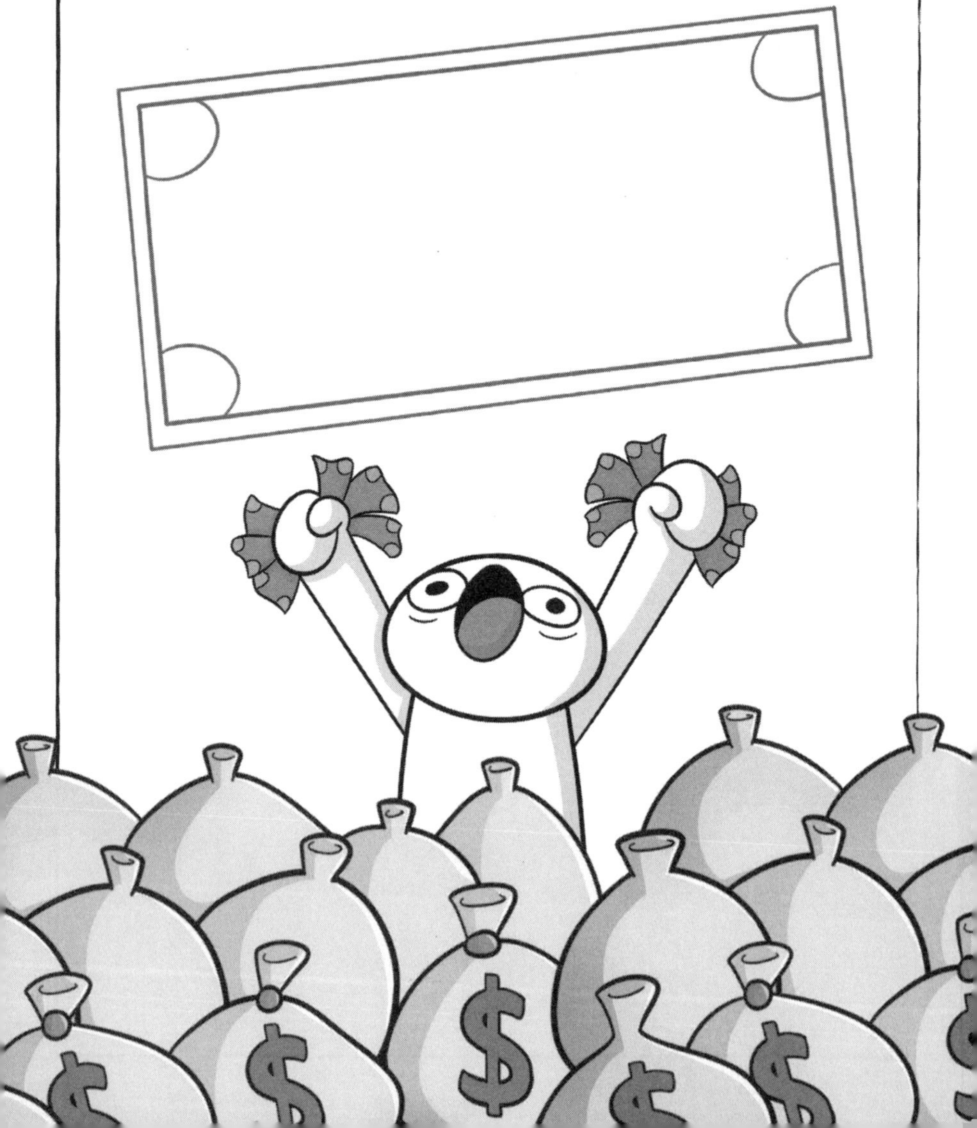

AND IN THE BLUE CORNER, WE HAVE THE UNDEFEATED

_____ !!!

Who is in the ring with James? Draw his opponent.

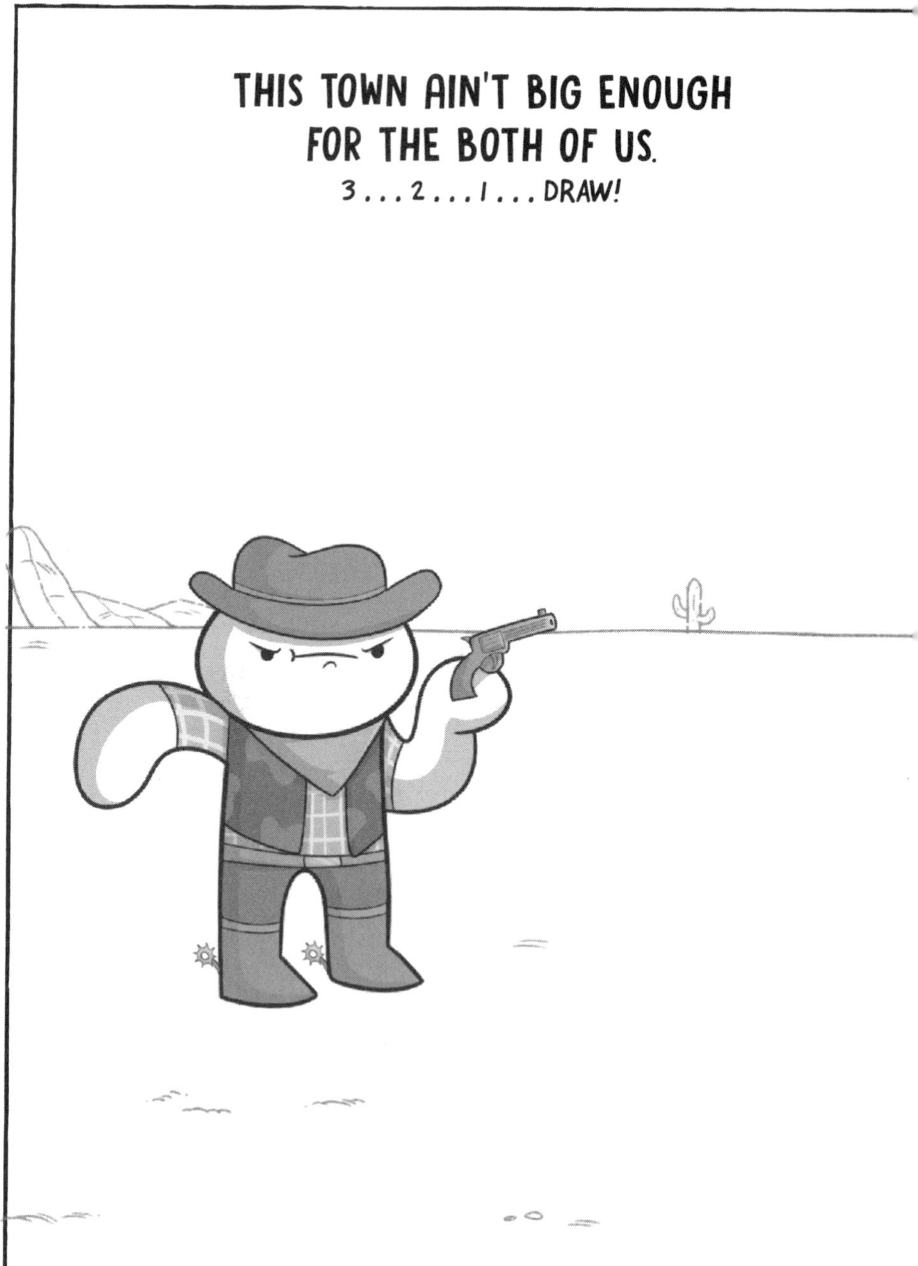
THIS TOWN AIN'T BIG ENOUGH FOR THE BOTH OF US.
3...2...1...DRAW!

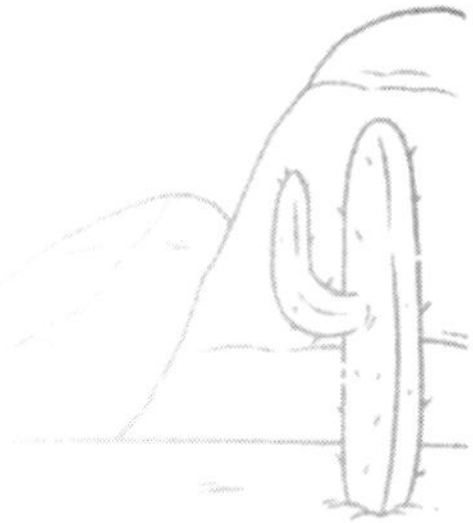

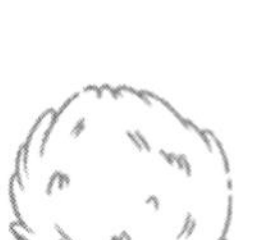

THE LIFE CYCLE OF HARRY THE MOTH

Harry the Moth may have had an untimely death in the beak of a bird, but his legacy will live on forever. So . . . maybe just draw a regular moth's life cycle.

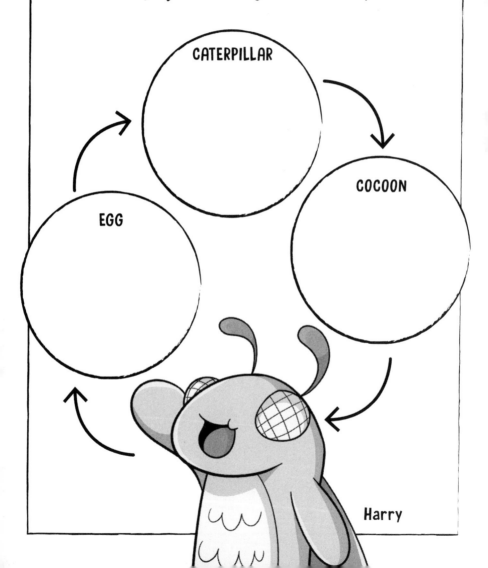

CATERPILLAR

COCOON

EGG

Harry

YOUR FINEST ACHIEVEMENTS

That's a nice collection of patches you have there! Fill them in with your proudest accomplishments.

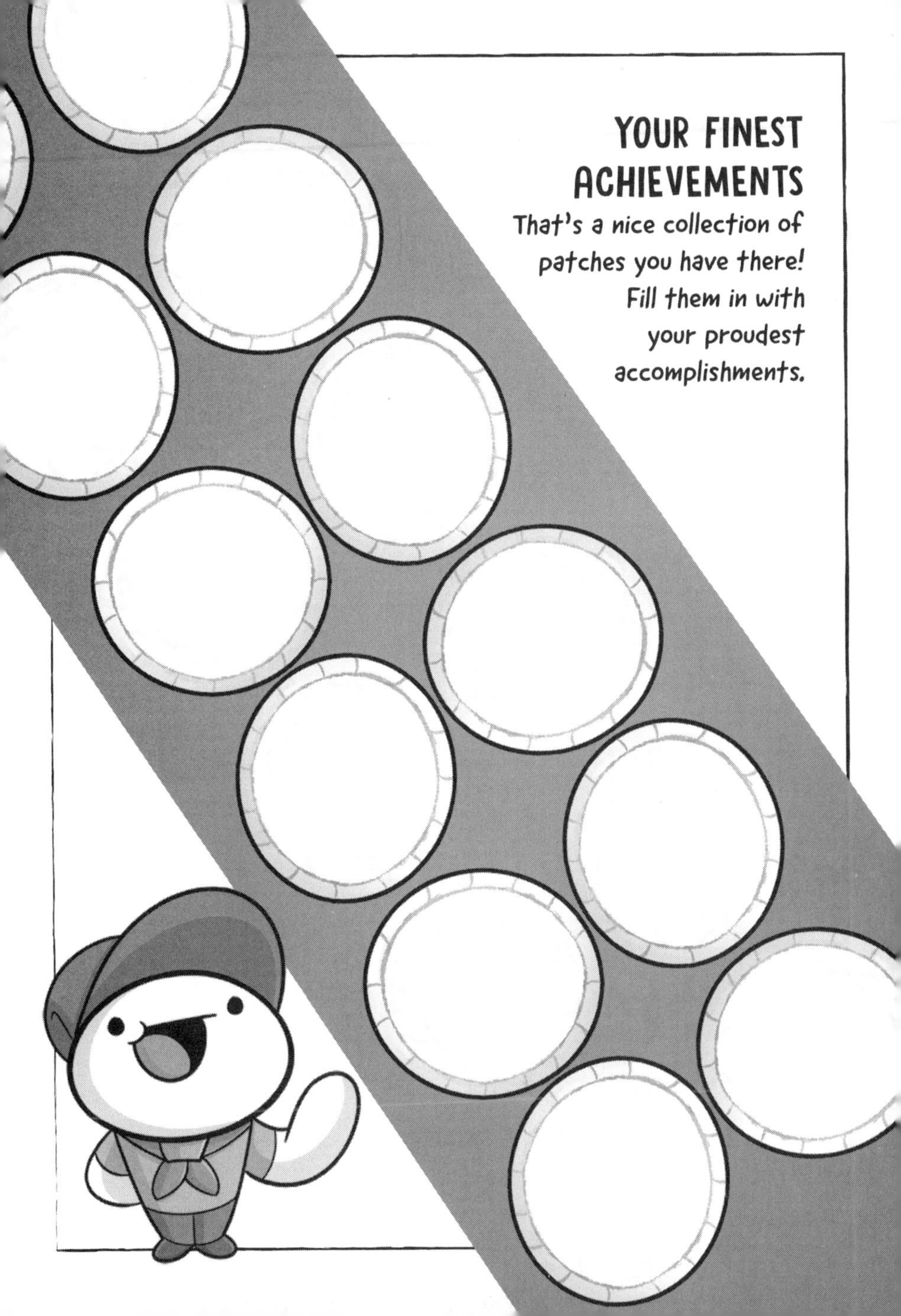

NOW SHOWING . . .

What do you want to see at the movies?
Design some movie posters!

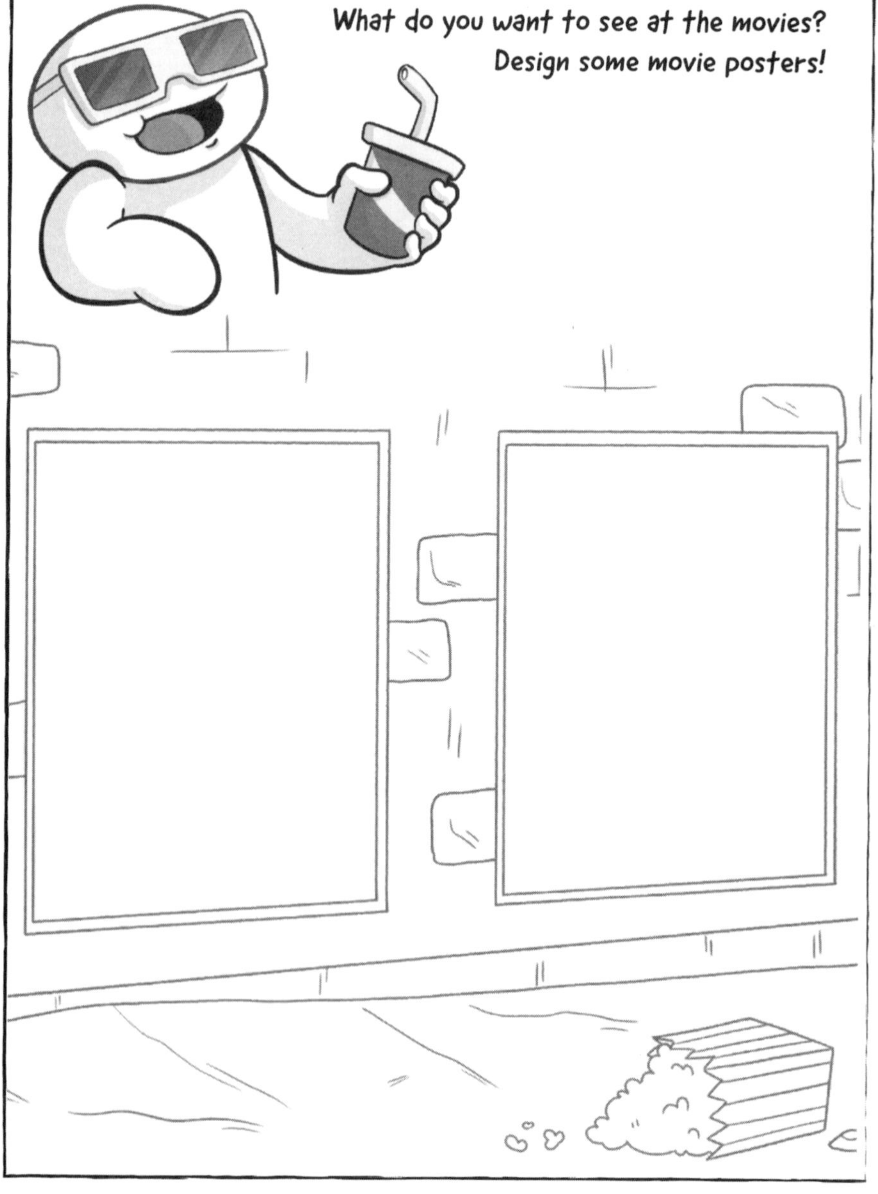

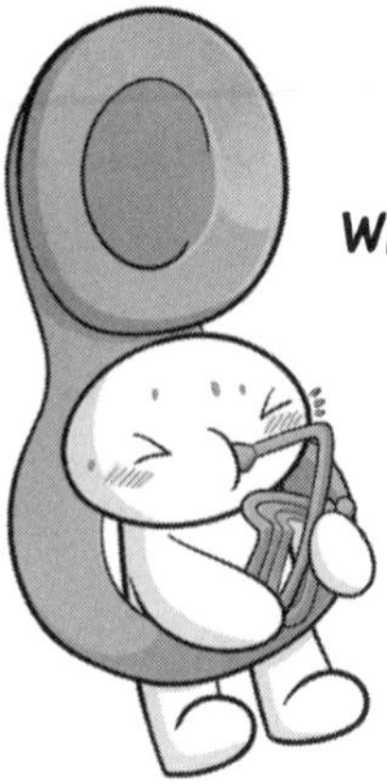

BAND AUDITIONS

James has got the tuba covered, kind of . . .
What instrument are you going to audition with?
Draw yourself playing a tune on it below.

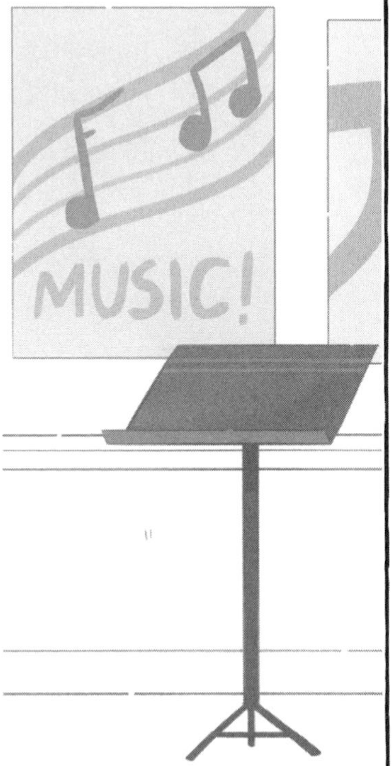
MUSIC!

EXTRA! EXTRA! READ ALL ABOUT . . .?

Draw today's headline on the newspaper.

NEWS

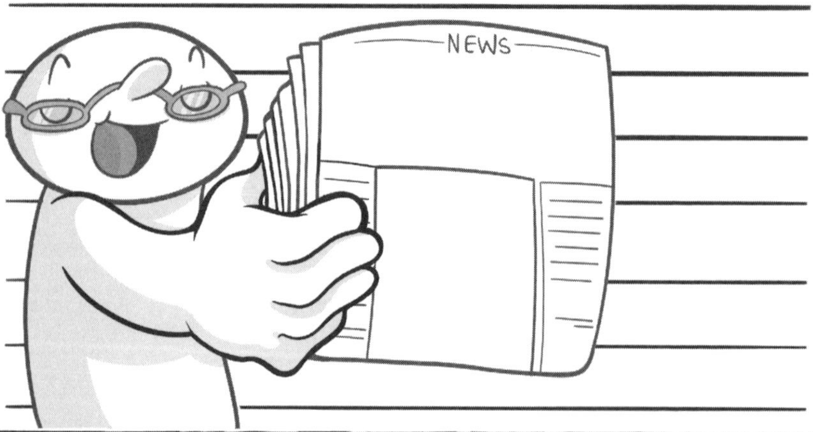
NEWS

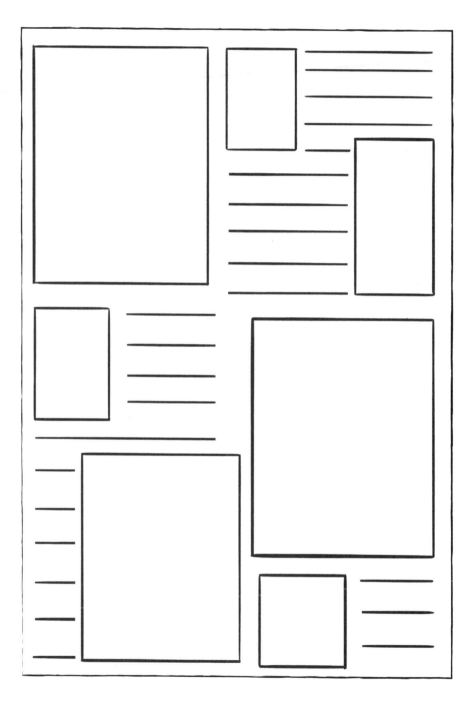

AND THUS I PRESENT TO YOU . . .

THE ______________________________ !

UHHH . . . YOU SPENT 15 YEARS ON THIS??

What has Professor Odd invented in his lab? Draw it below.

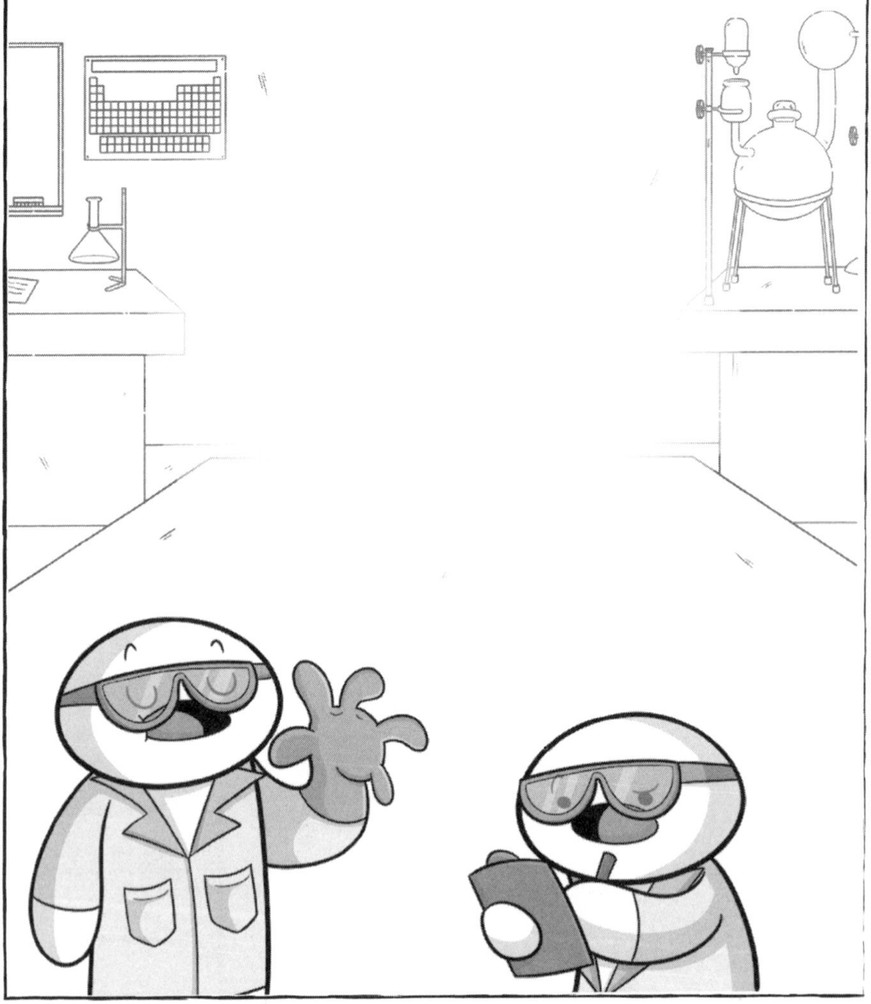

OH NO! HE DREW ON THE WALLS AGAIN??

This little guy got creative on the wall with a crayon.
Help him finish this maze!

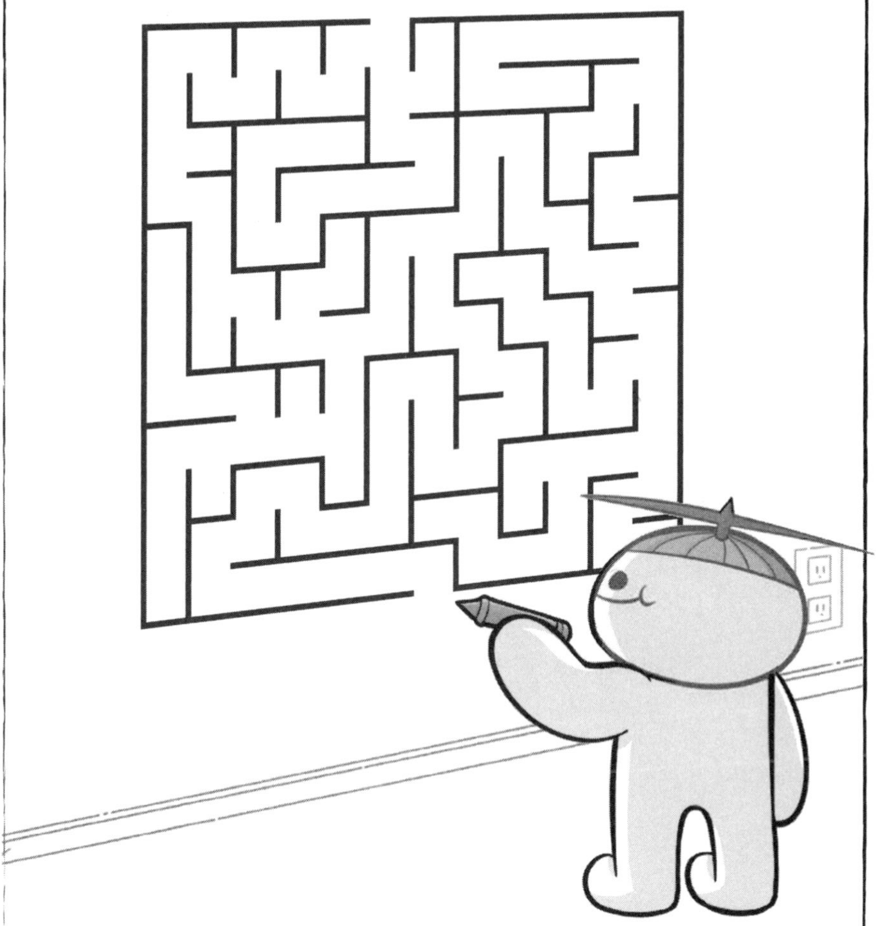

CELEBRITY SIGHTING!

Everyone wants to meet this V.I.P.!
Who's waiting in line? Draw them below.

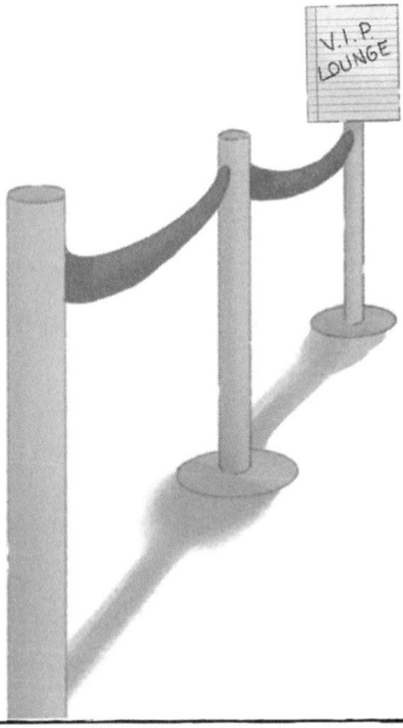
V.I.P.
LOUNGE

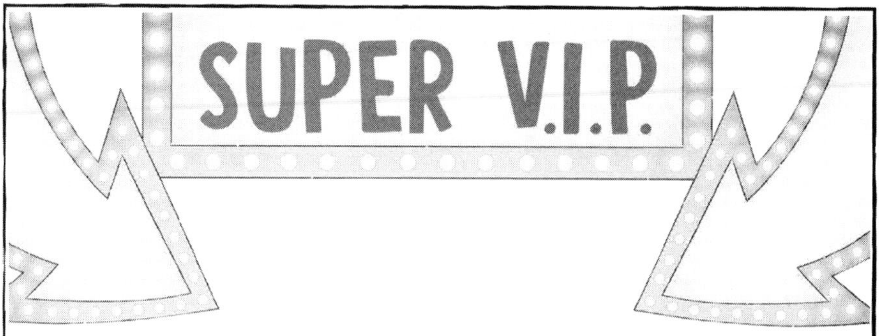
SUPER V.I.P.

Who's everyone waiting to see?
Draw this very important person!

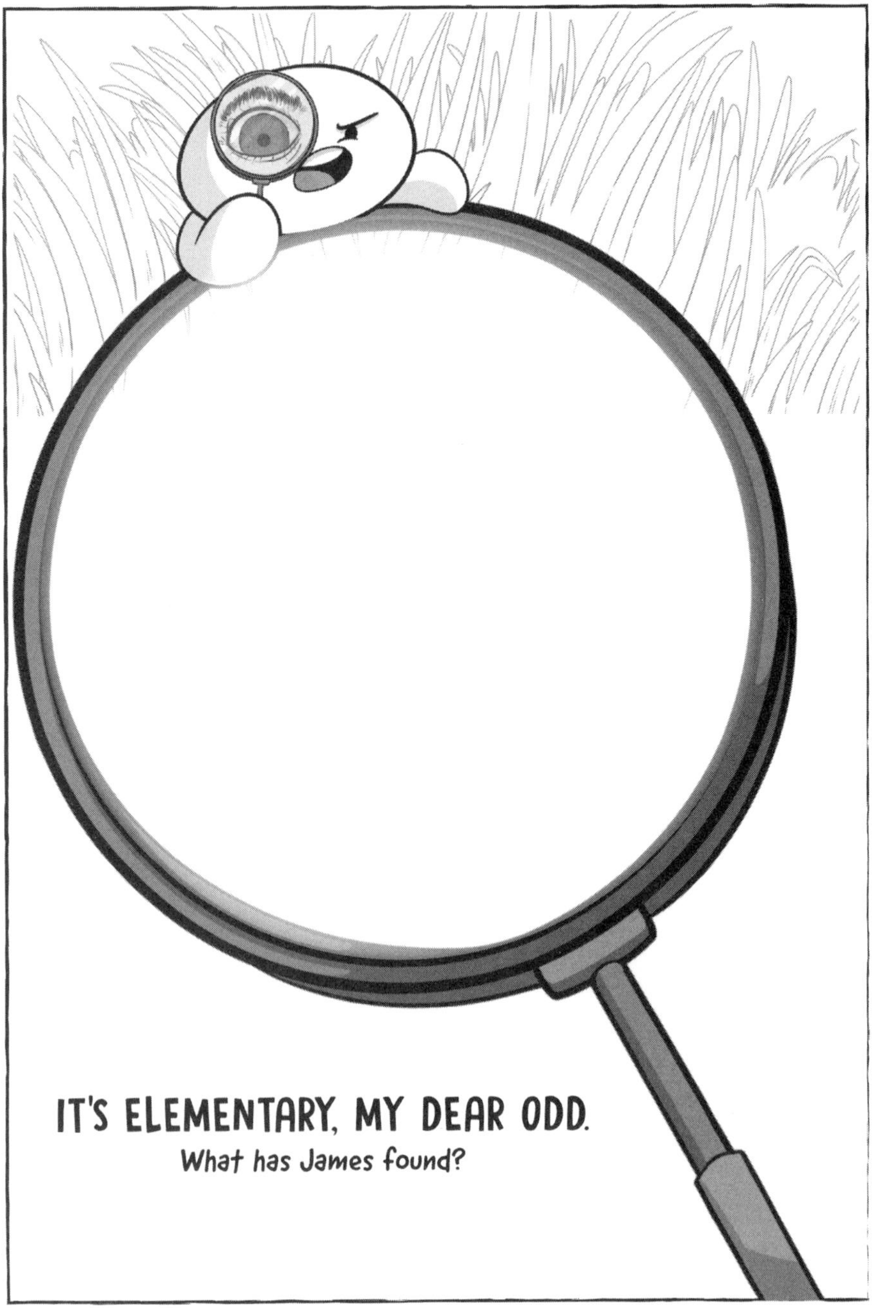
IT'S ELEMENTARY, MY DEAR ODD.
What has James found?

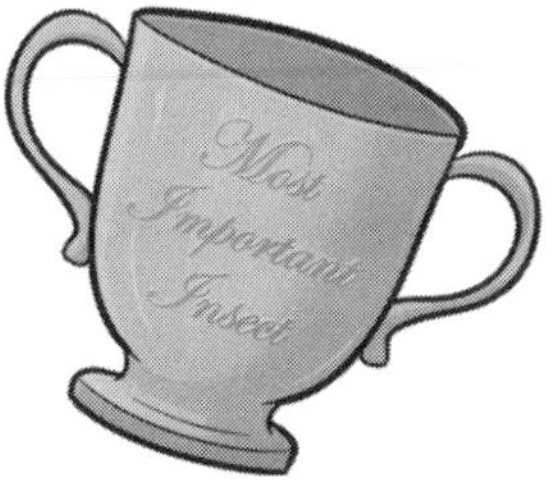
Most
Important
Insect

WELCOME TO THE MOST IMPORTANT INSECT AWARDS.

Who will take home the trophy?
Draw them on the podium in first place.

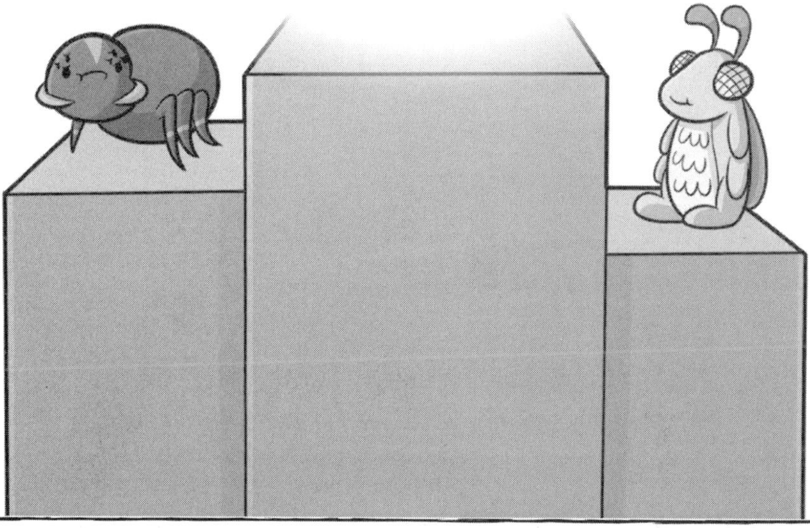

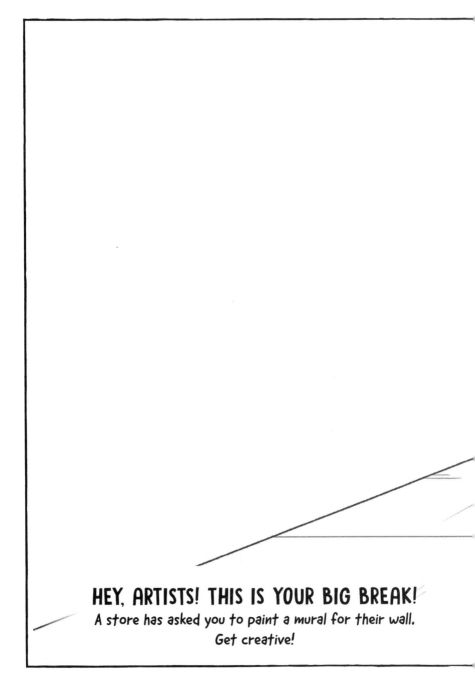

HEY, ARTISTS! THIS IS YOUR BIG BREAK!
A store has asked you to paint a mural for their wall.
Get creative!

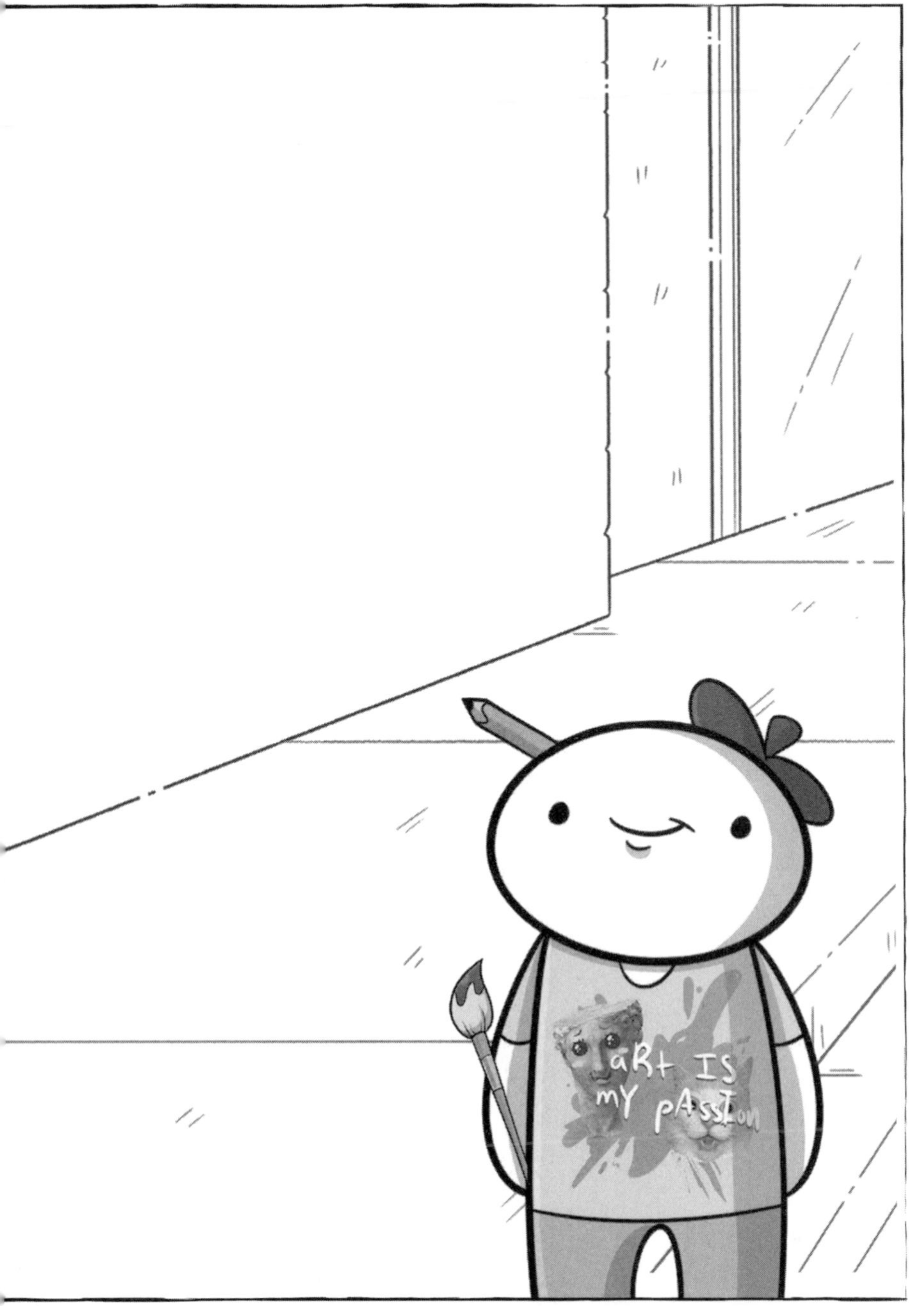
aRt IS
my pASSIon

IT'S NOT A PHASE, MOM!

This teenage rebel wants to stand out from the crowd.
Give him an edgy outfit. The more skulls, the better!

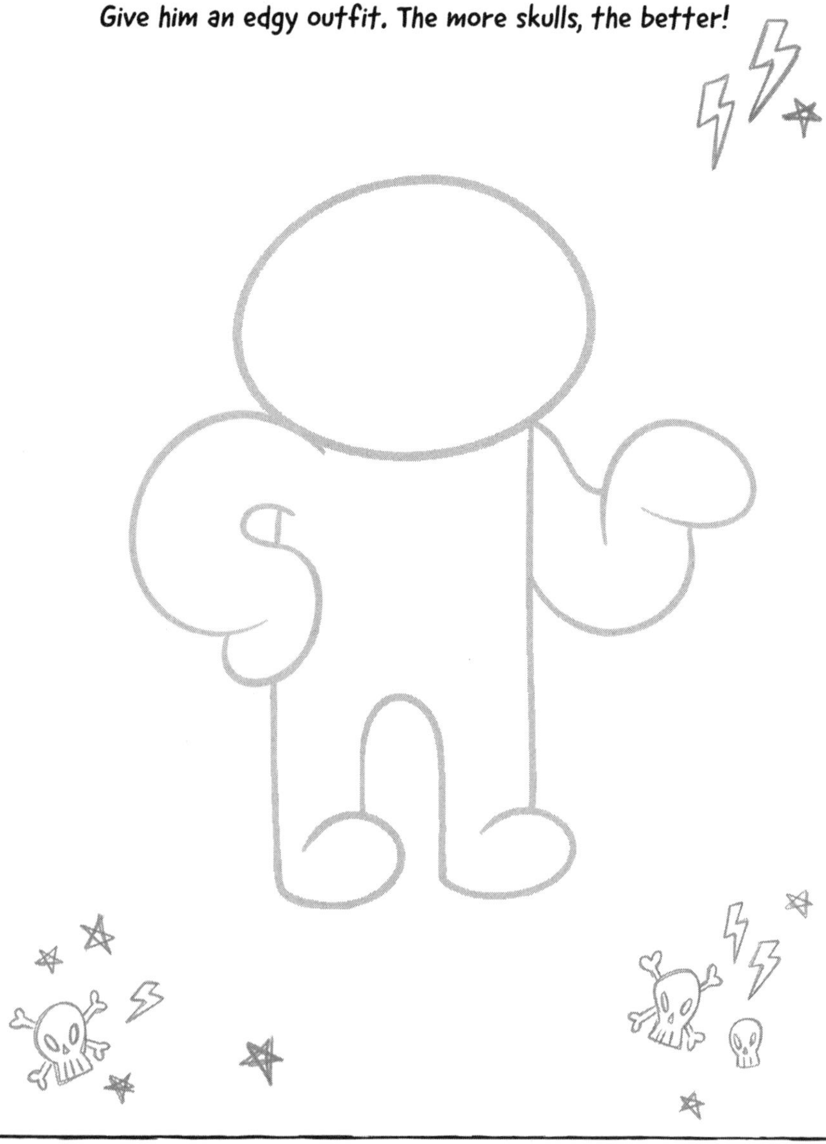

NO, YOU HANG UP FIRST!

Odd is on the phone with a crush.
Draw who they're talking to!

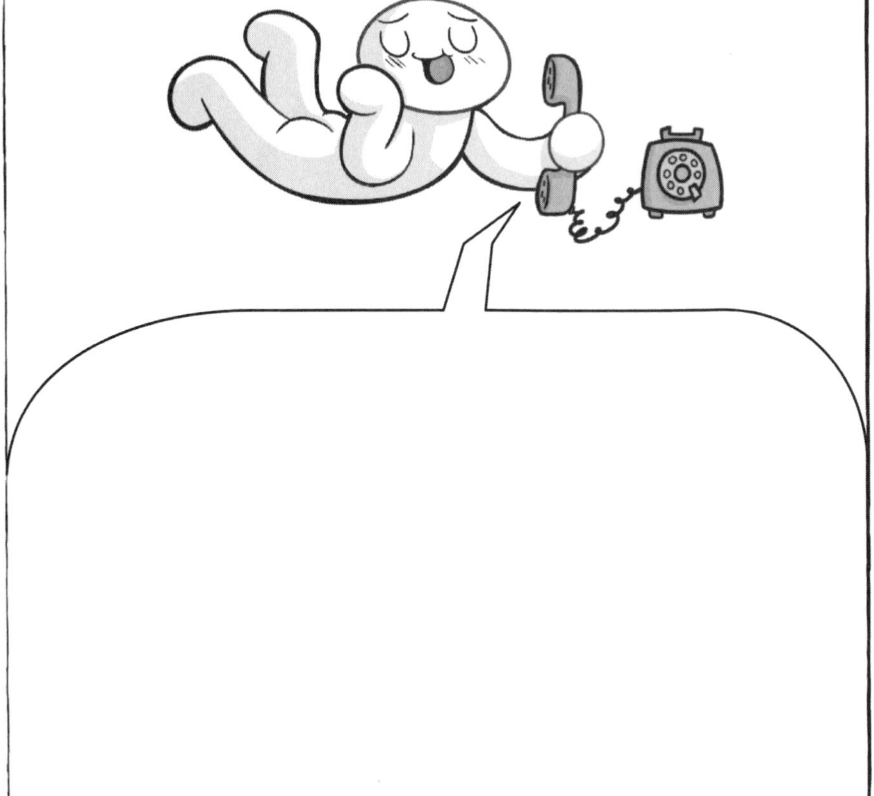

SNOW MUCH FUN!

Look at this cool snowman! But wait, where are his face and clothes? Help this poor guy out, dear doodler!

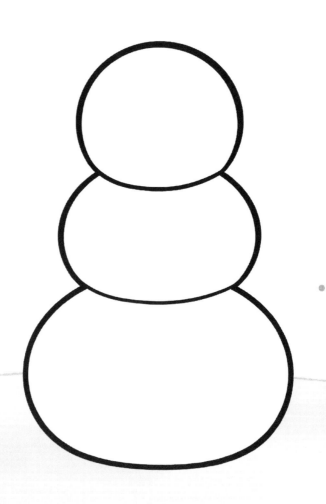

BRRR-ILLIANT!

What crazy snow creation has James built? Draw it below!

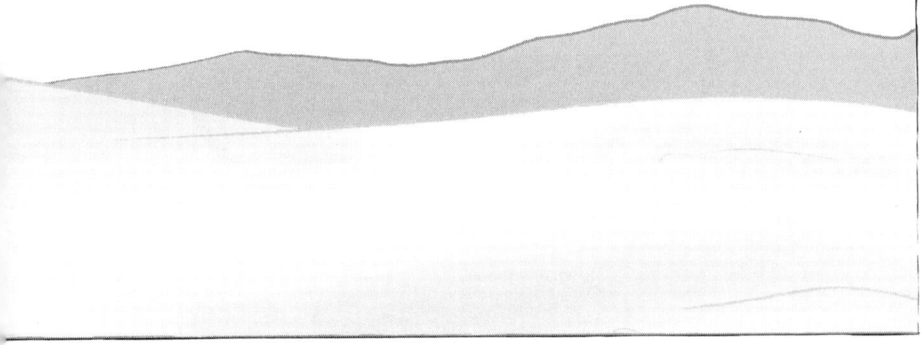

AND IN FIRST PLACE IS . . .
WAIT, WHO IS THAT?!
And what on Earth are they driving?!

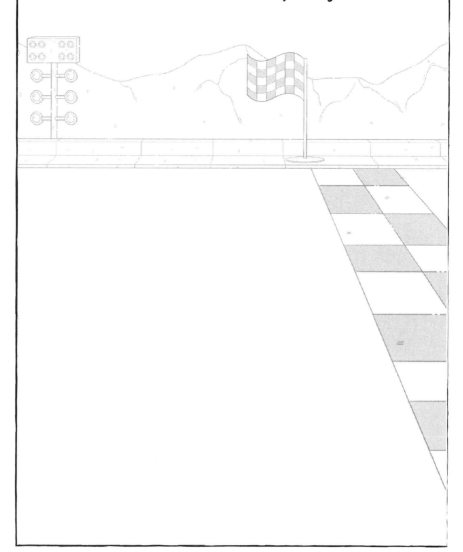

NOT-QUITE-A-DEATH-MATCH

These monsters could be here all day and they wouldn't hurt a fly. Are they tired or just useless? Draw who's fighting.

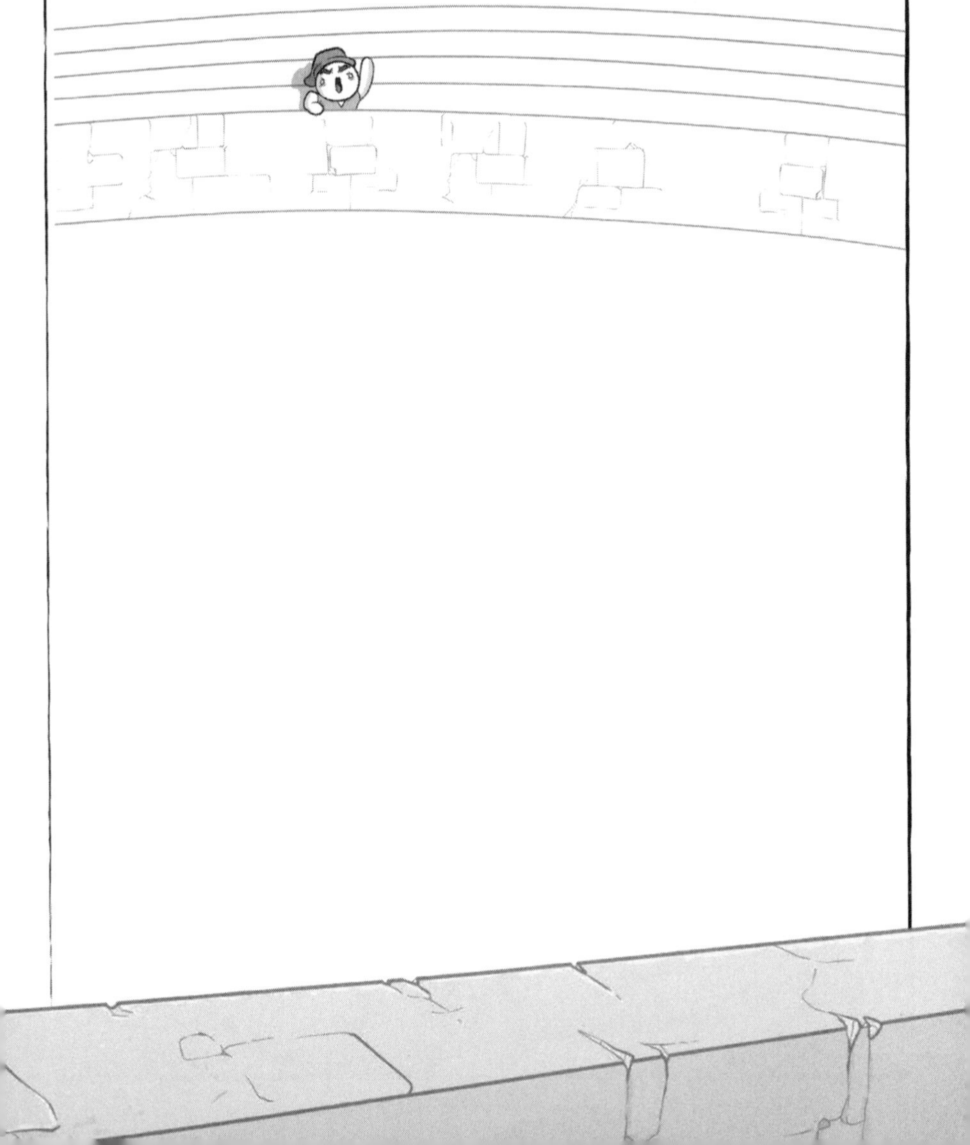

ARE YOU A CAT PERSON
OR A DOG PERSON?
Doodle your choice below!

HEY! YOU CAN'T HIDE IN THERE FOREVER!
This creature has disappeared inside their shell!
Have a go at <u>drawing</u> them out!

THE BUS IS LATE AGAIN!
IT WOULDN'T BE SO BAD IF I WASN'T
STUCK WITH THESE WEIRDOS.
Who (or what) is waiting with James at the bus stop?

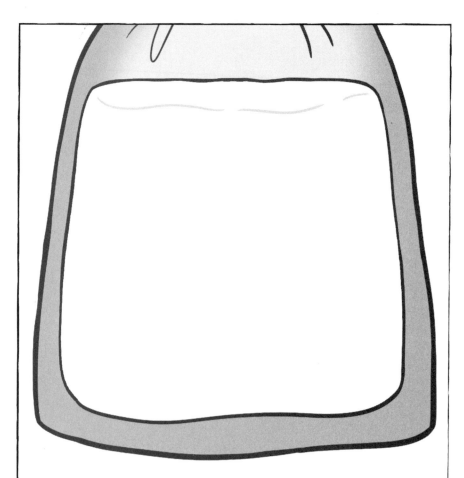

**MOM!
CHECK OUT THIS FISH!**
Honey, you need to return that to the pet shop! I don't know what that is, but it ISN'T a fish.

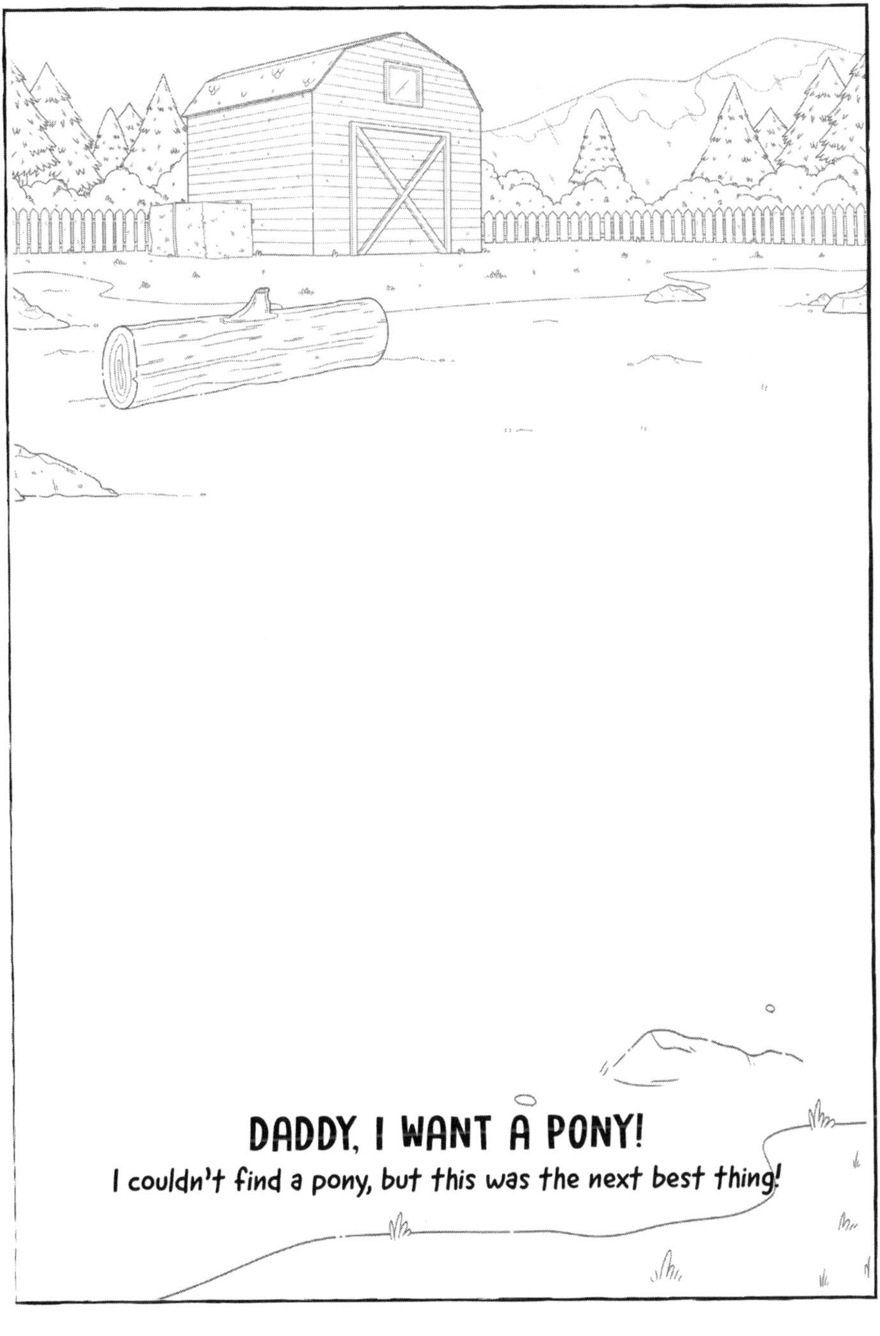

DADDY, I WANT A PONY!

I couldn't find a pony, but this was the next best thing!

WHOA! A MONSTER THAT SCARED THE MONSTERS?!

Draw the monster that has scared these goons.

SWEET DREAMS, LITTLE SPIDER.

What do spiders dream about anyway?
Draw what this young arachnid is dreaming about.

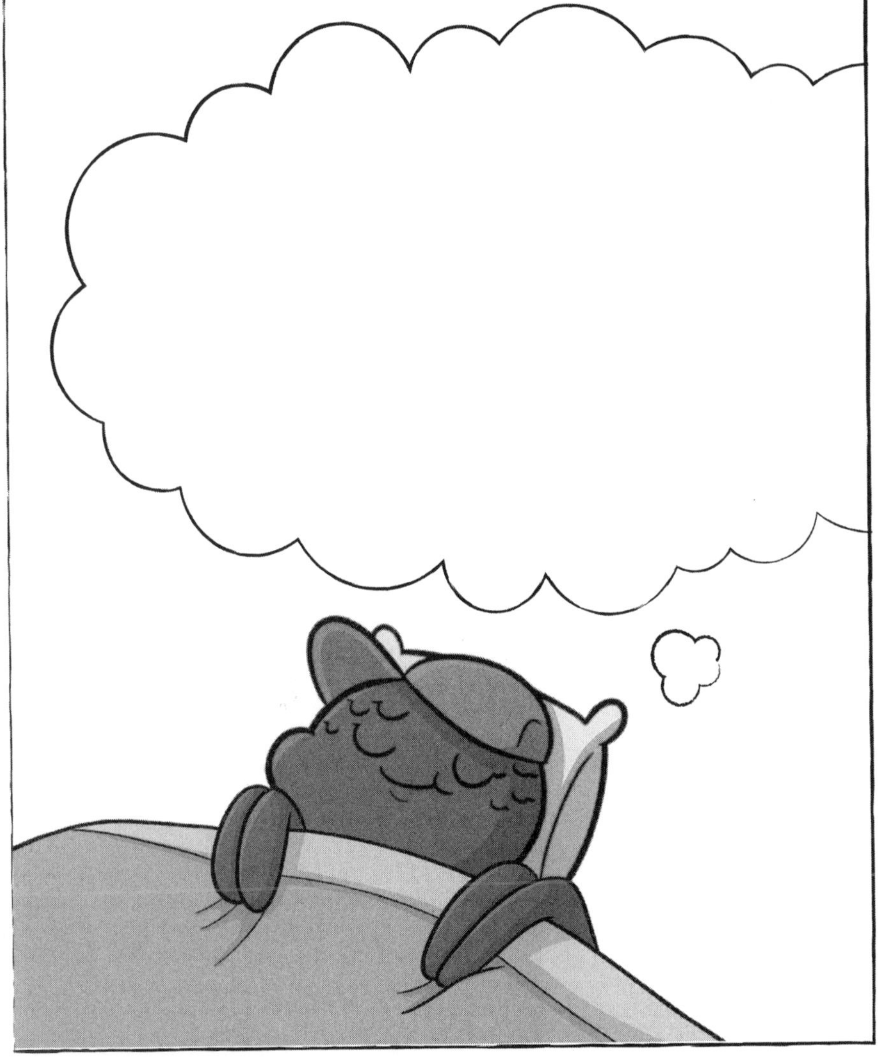

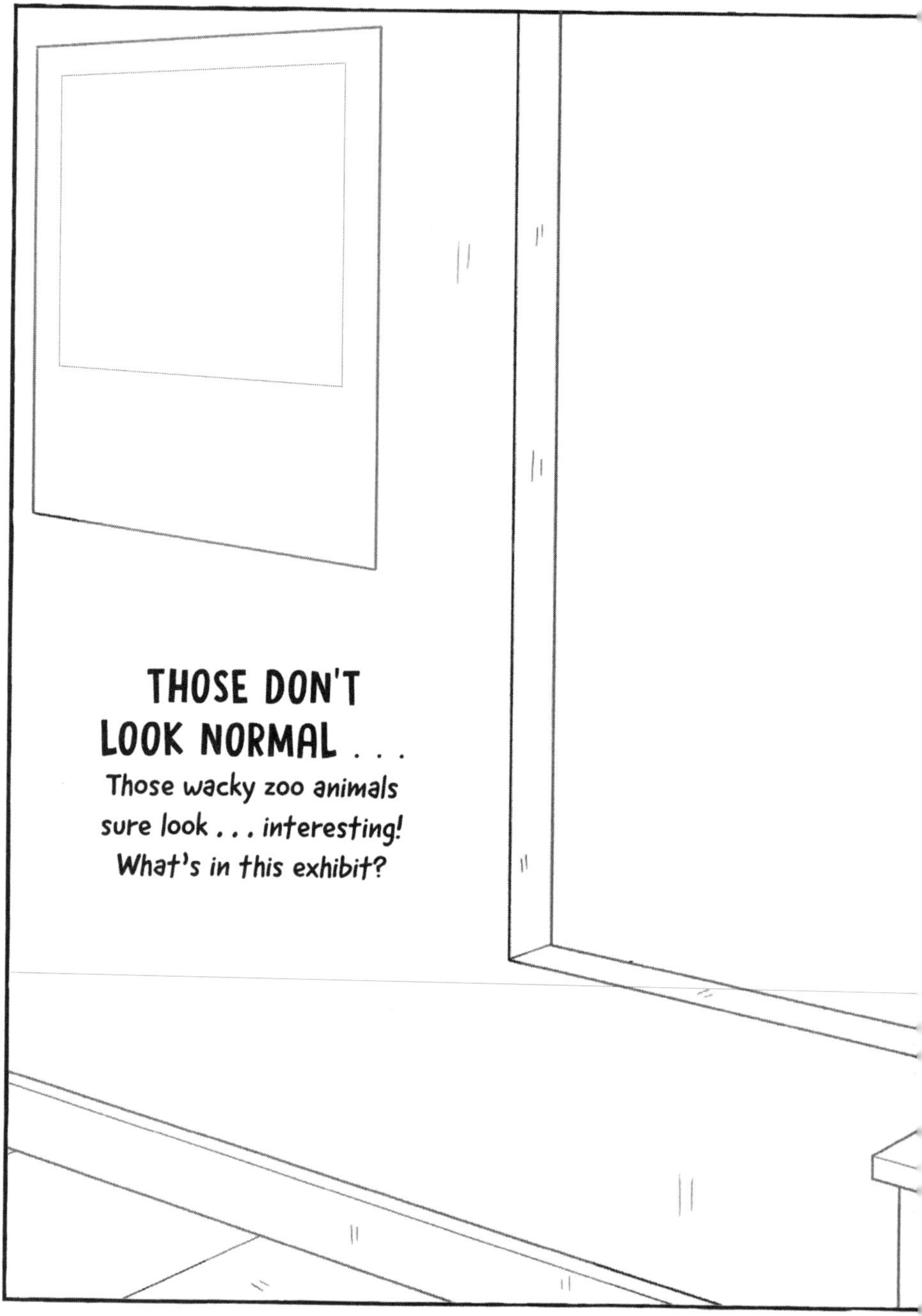
THOSE DON'T LOOK NORMAL . . .
Those wacky zoo animals sure look . . . interesting! What's in this exhibit?

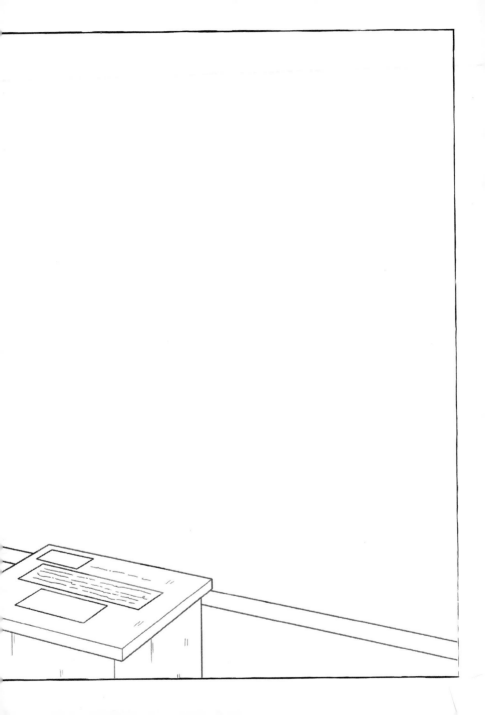

ADD A HORN, YOU GET A ________ CORN!

Pretty simple: make your own unicorn hybrids below.

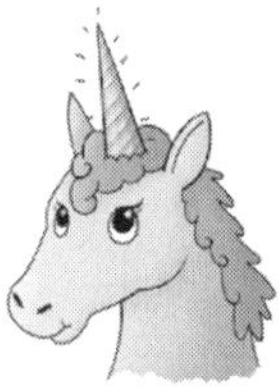

UNICORN

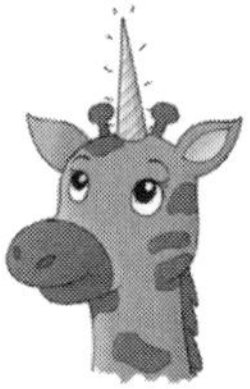

GIRAFFECORN

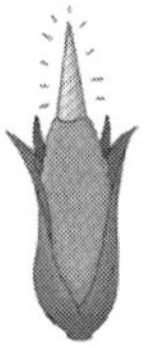

CORNCORN

AW, A RAINBOW! AND I CAN SEE THE END!

What is really at the end of the rainbow? Draw it below.
(Maybe add the rainbow, too!)

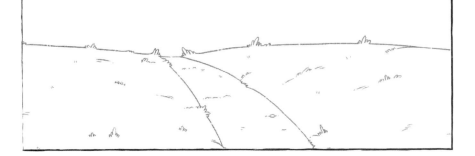

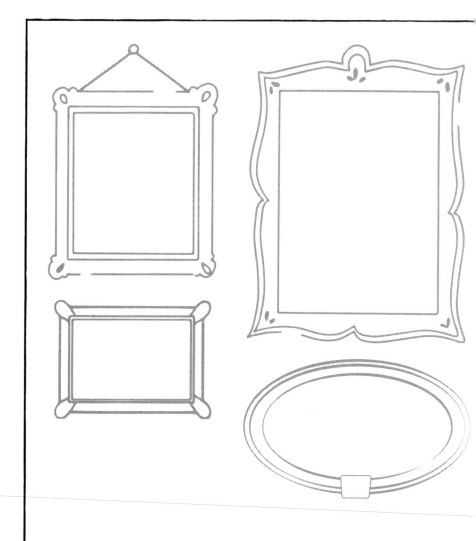

SO FANCY!
What amazing (and expensive) works
of art are in these frames?

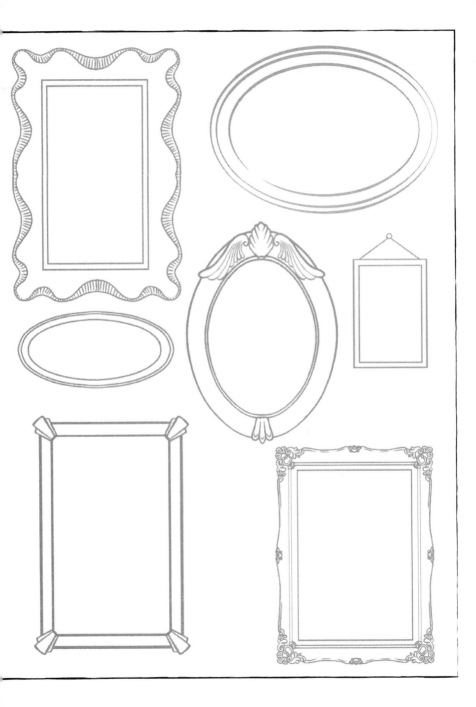

I KNEW THIS SHORTCUT WAS A BAD IDEA . . .

What's blocking the road ahead? Draw it.

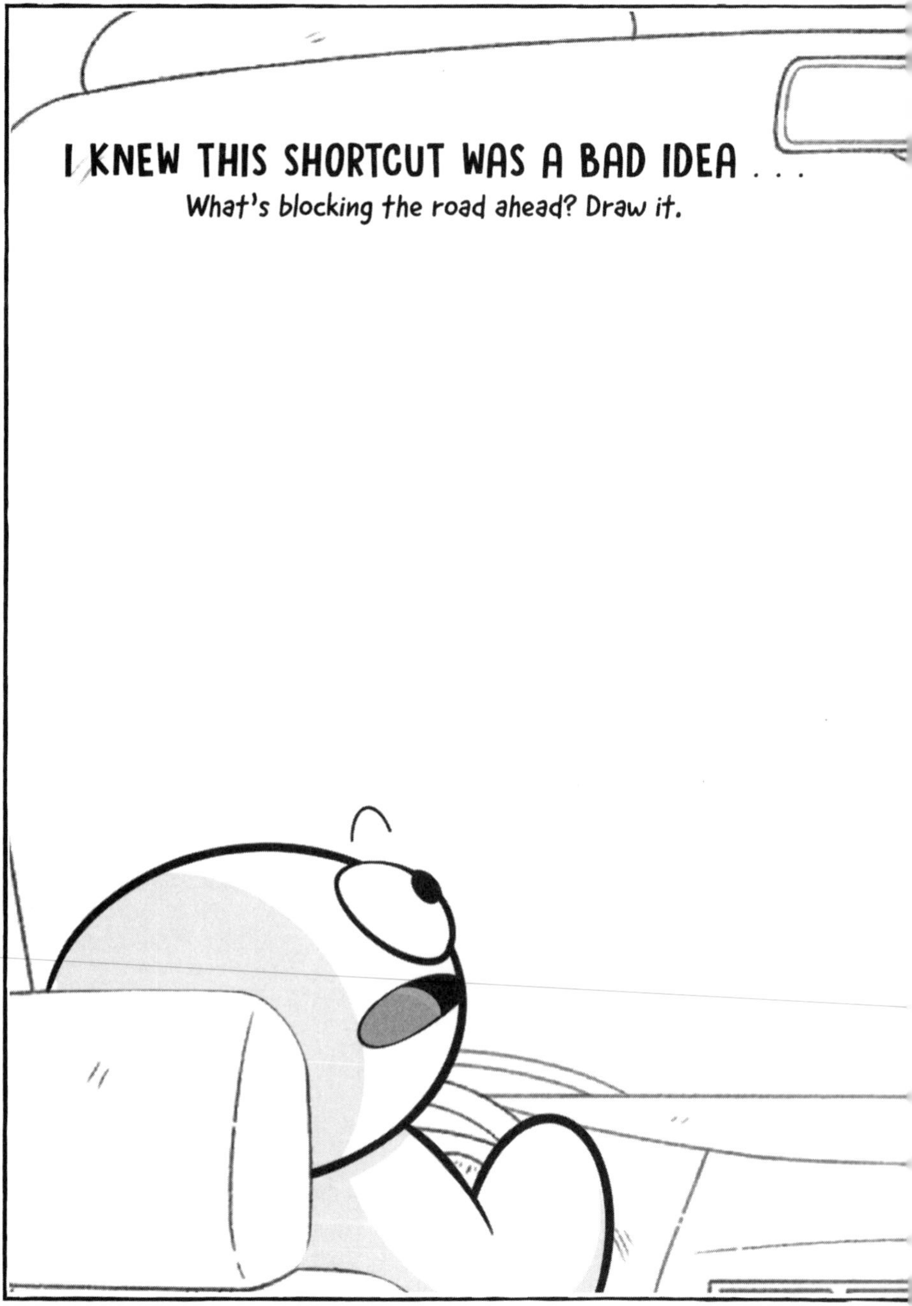

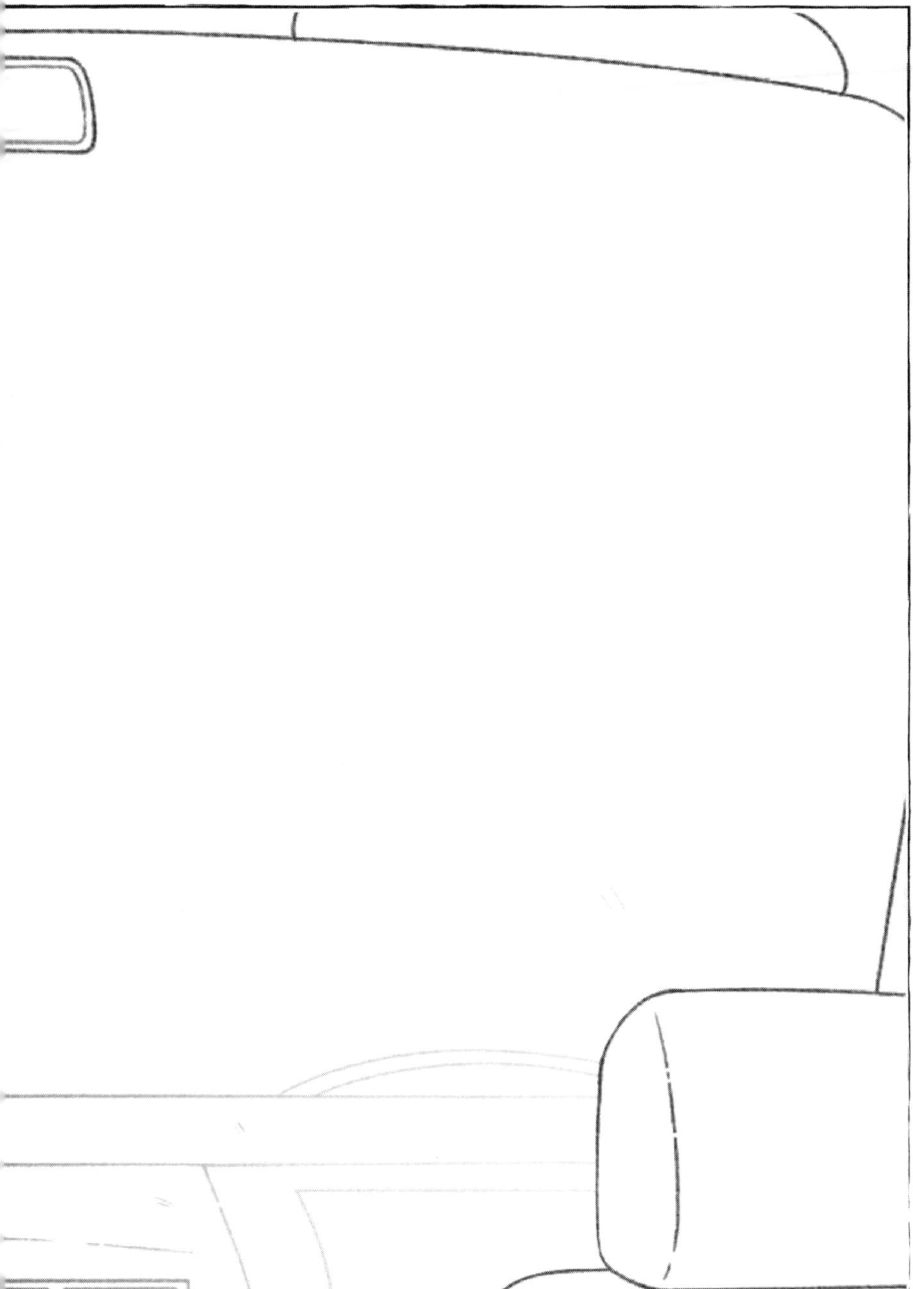

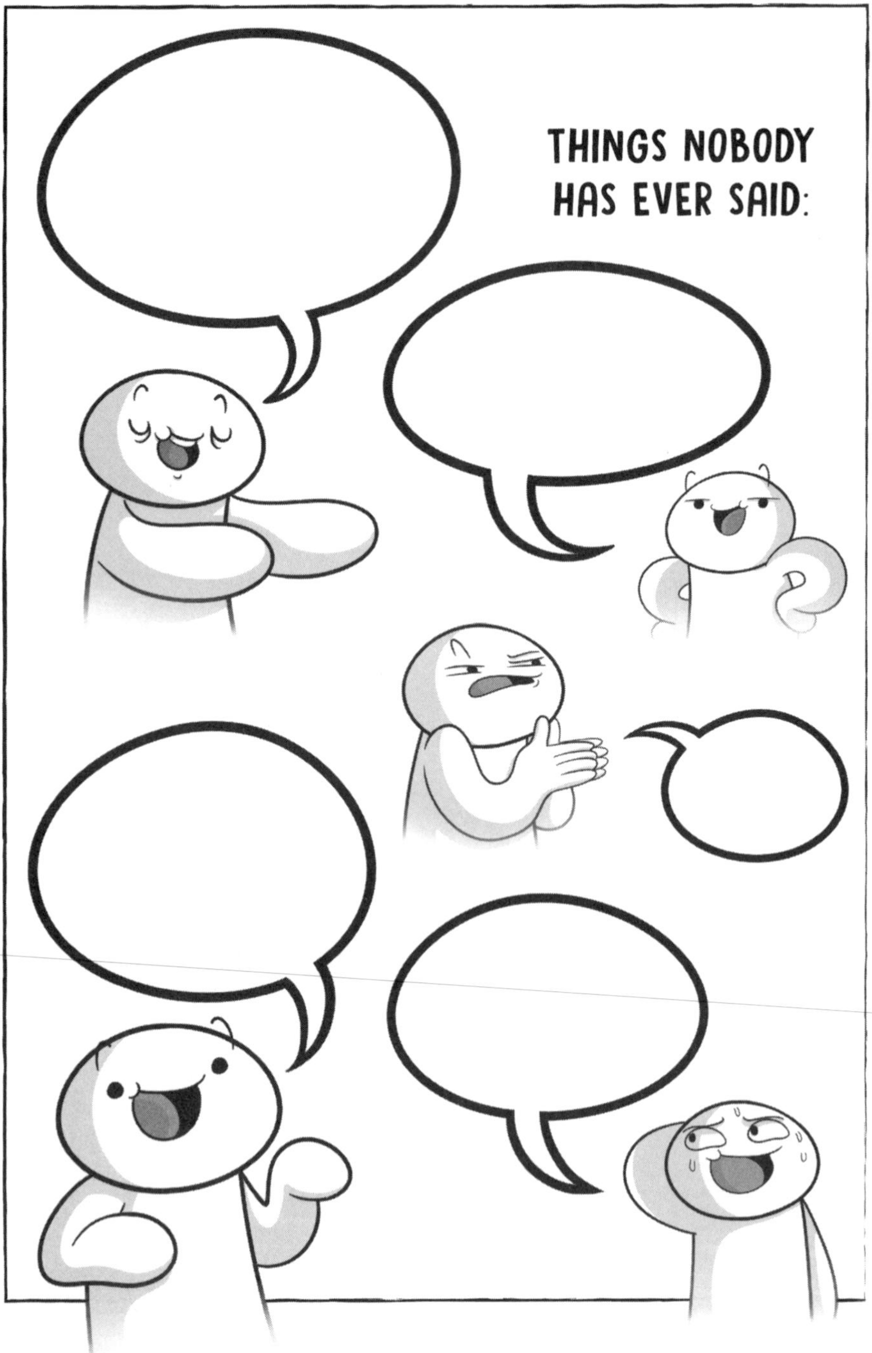
THINGS NOBODY HAS EVER SAID:

DO YOU EVEN LIKE SNOW GLOBES?

Draw your collection.

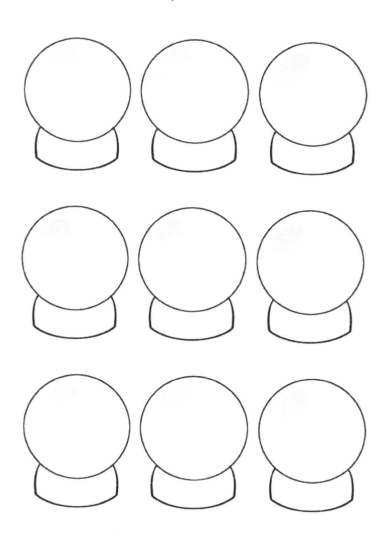

REEL IT IN!
What has James got on the end of his fishing line?

I DUNNO IF THAT'S GONNA FLOAT . . .
It will float if you say it's gonna float!
Design your dream pool floaty!

ALL AROUND ME ARE
FREAKY FACES . . .
Go on, give these freaky faces some freaky bodies!

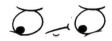

SO YOU WANNA BE AN INFLUENCER?!

Let's see what you've got!
Design a thumbnail for your video.
Don't forget to add a title!

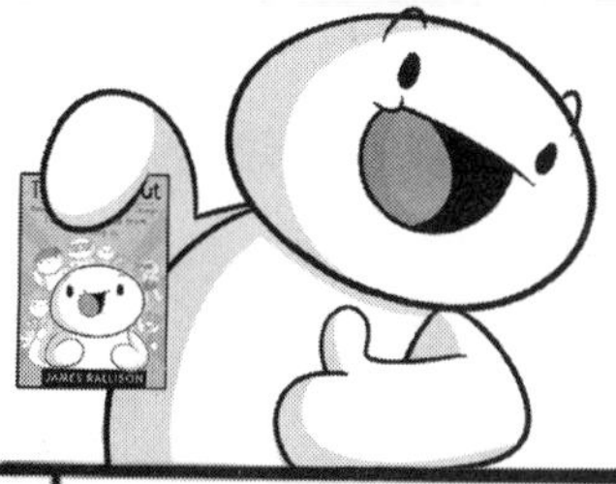

WE GET IT! YOU WROTE A BOOK!

Why don't you design the cover for the next Odd Is Out book?

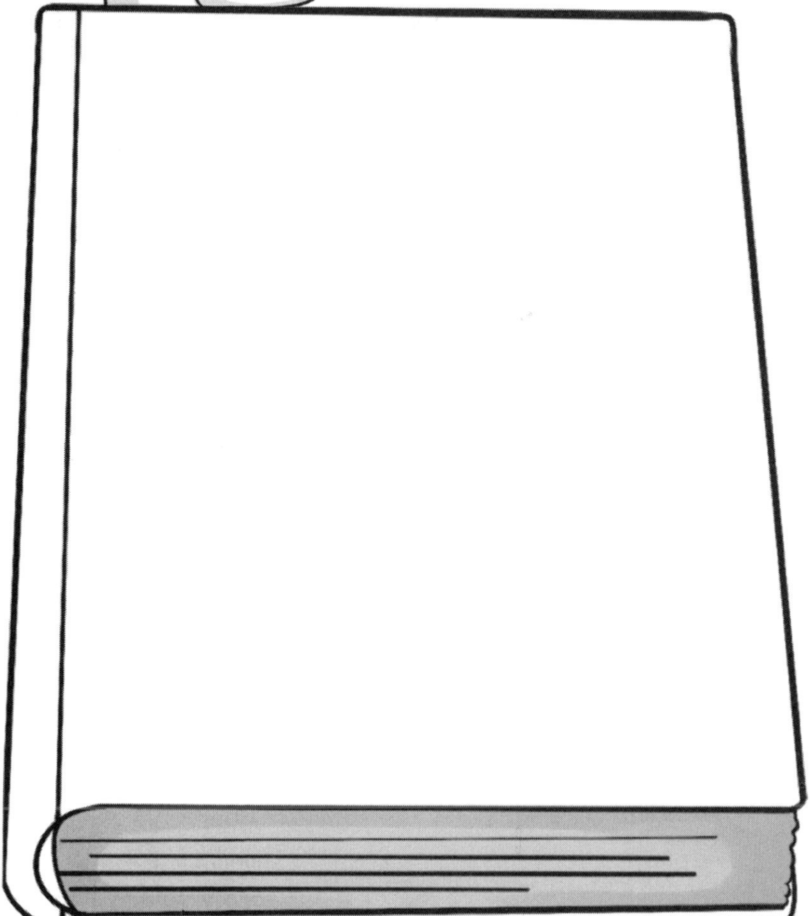

IT'S A BIRD! IT'S A PLANE! IT'S A . . . WHAT???

What is coming over the horizon?

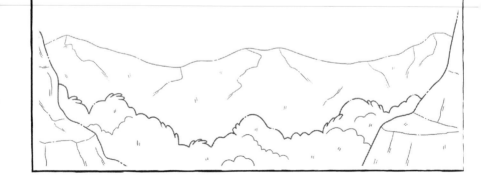

YES! A SUPERHERO IS HERE TO SAVE THE DAY!

No, not you, James—you're wearing boxers and a bedsheet.
I mean you, Captain Doodler! Design your super suit below.

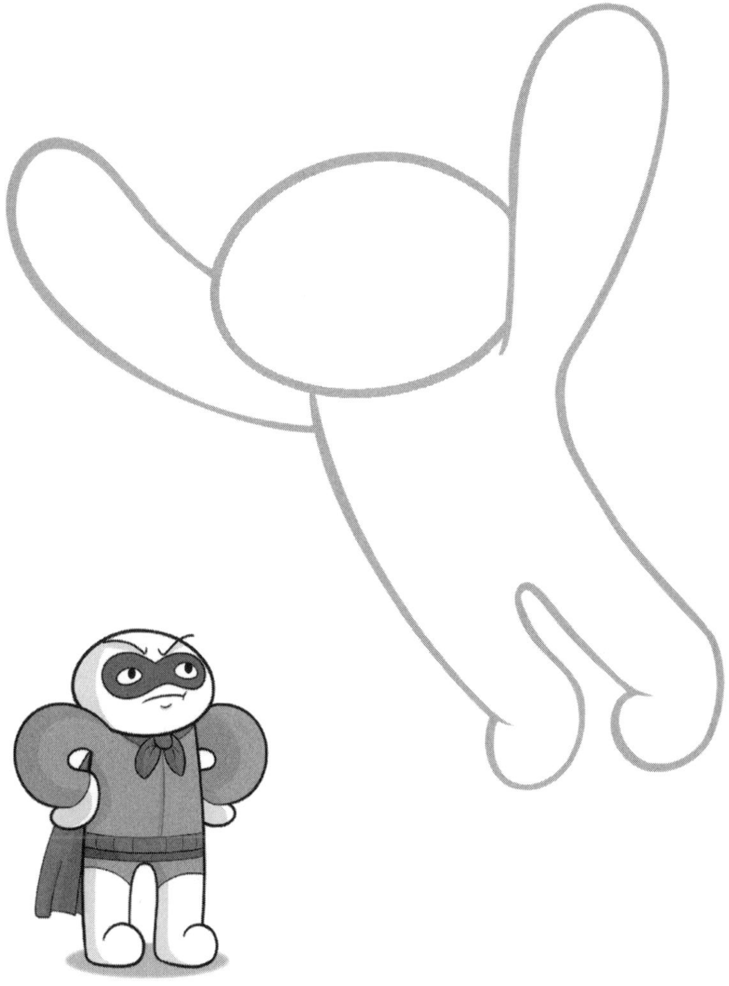

JAMES HAS A BIG DECISION TO MAKE. WILL HE LISTEN TO THE ANGEL ON HIS SHOULDER?

Draw an angel on James's shoulder.

OR HIS DEVIL?
Draw a devil on James's shoulder.

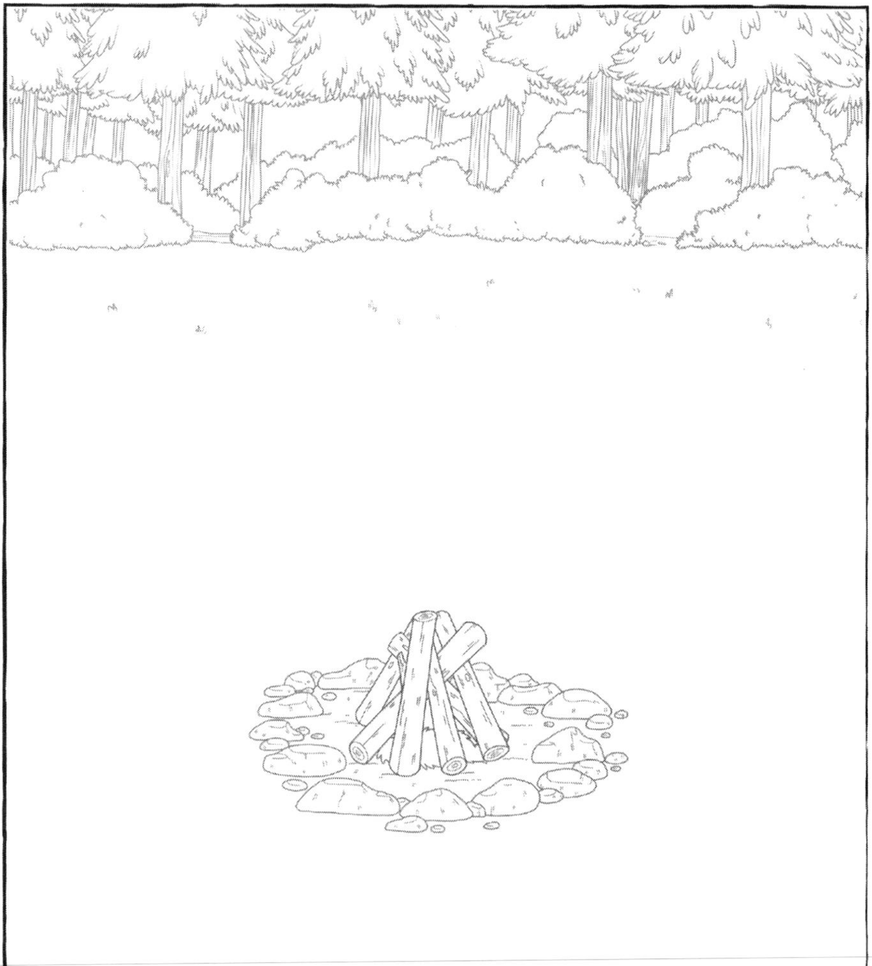

IT'S THE SIMPLE THINGS IN LIFE:

A warm fire, good company,
that strange feeling you're being watched . . .
Who's gathered around the fire?

IT'S A MONSTER MASH!
What kind of scary creatures are at this
monster get-together?

**WOW, A MERMAID!
WAIT, WHERE'S YOUR TAIL?**
Draw this mermaid's tail!

MAN, WE'RE NEVER GONNA GET OUTTA HERE!

Who is stranded on this deserted island?

DRAW YOUR
HAPPY PLACE.
Fill this page with things
that make you feel
peaceful.

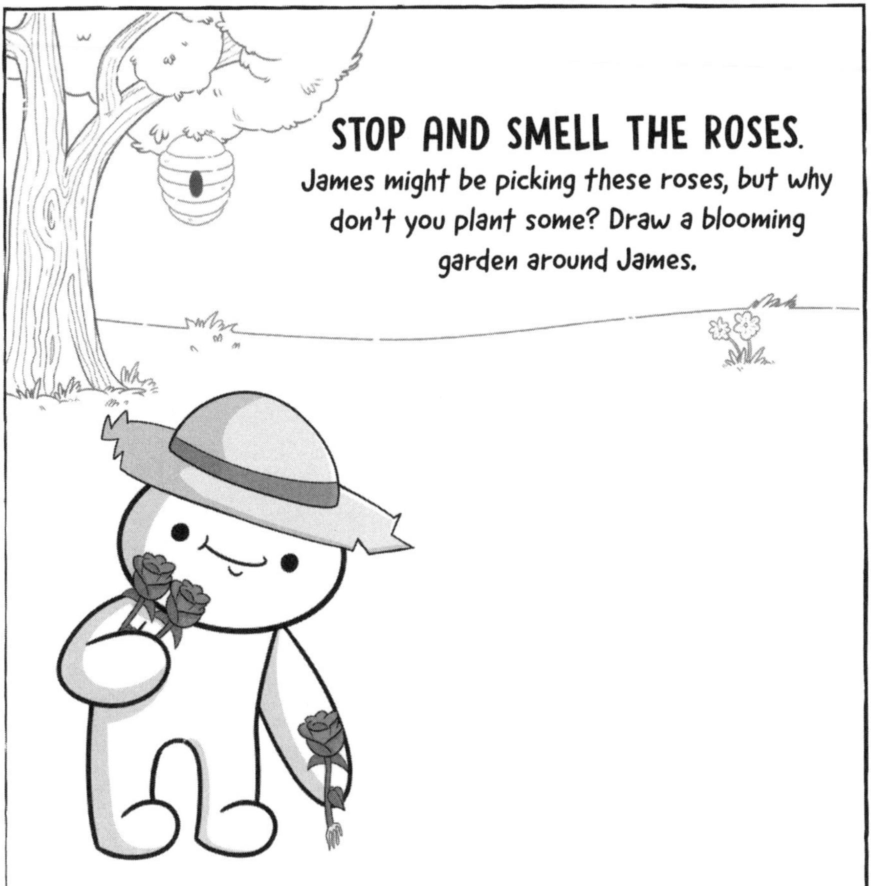

STOP AND SMELL THE ROSES.

James might be picking these roses, but why don't you plant some? Draw a blooming garden around James.

Certificate of Bossness
Awarded to:
_____

Awarded by
James Rallison

CEO OF ODDNESS
Who's in charge?

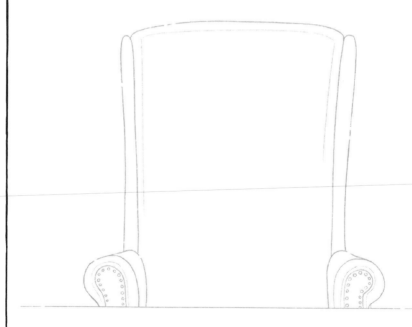

HERE WE ARE, YOUR BRAIN'S HEADQUARTERS.

Wait, where is everybody? Quick! Better put someone in charge!
Try decorating the place, too. It looks a bit empty.

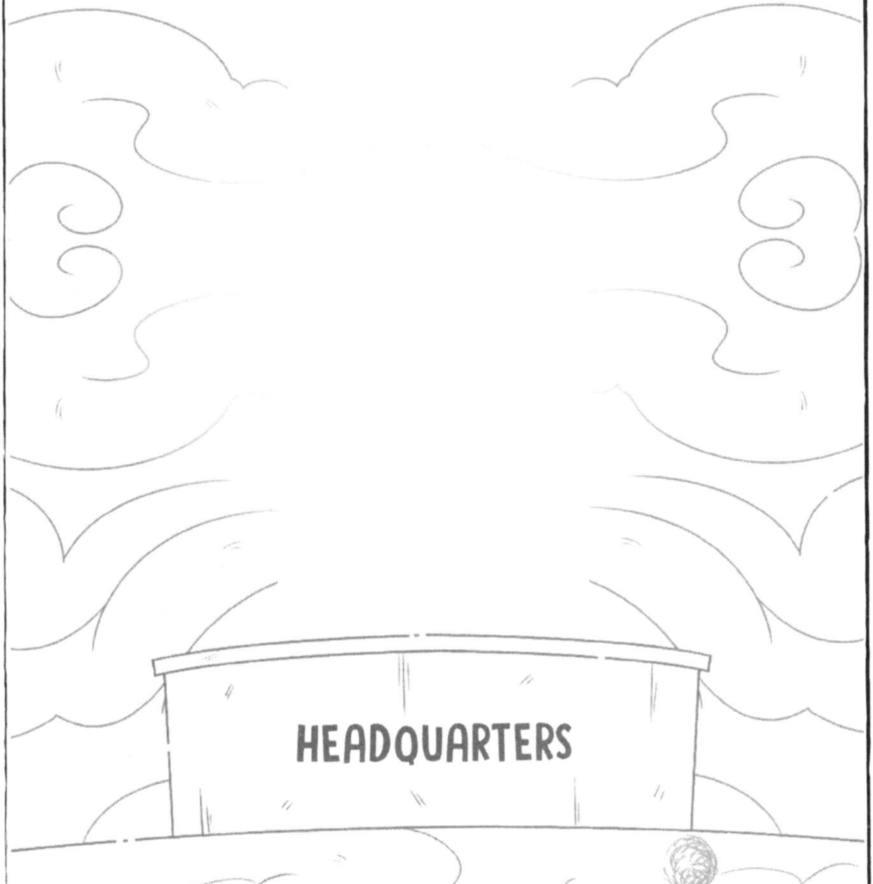
HEADQUARTERS

DINO BUDDIES

What kind of dinosaur is keeping this little guy company? Draw them below!

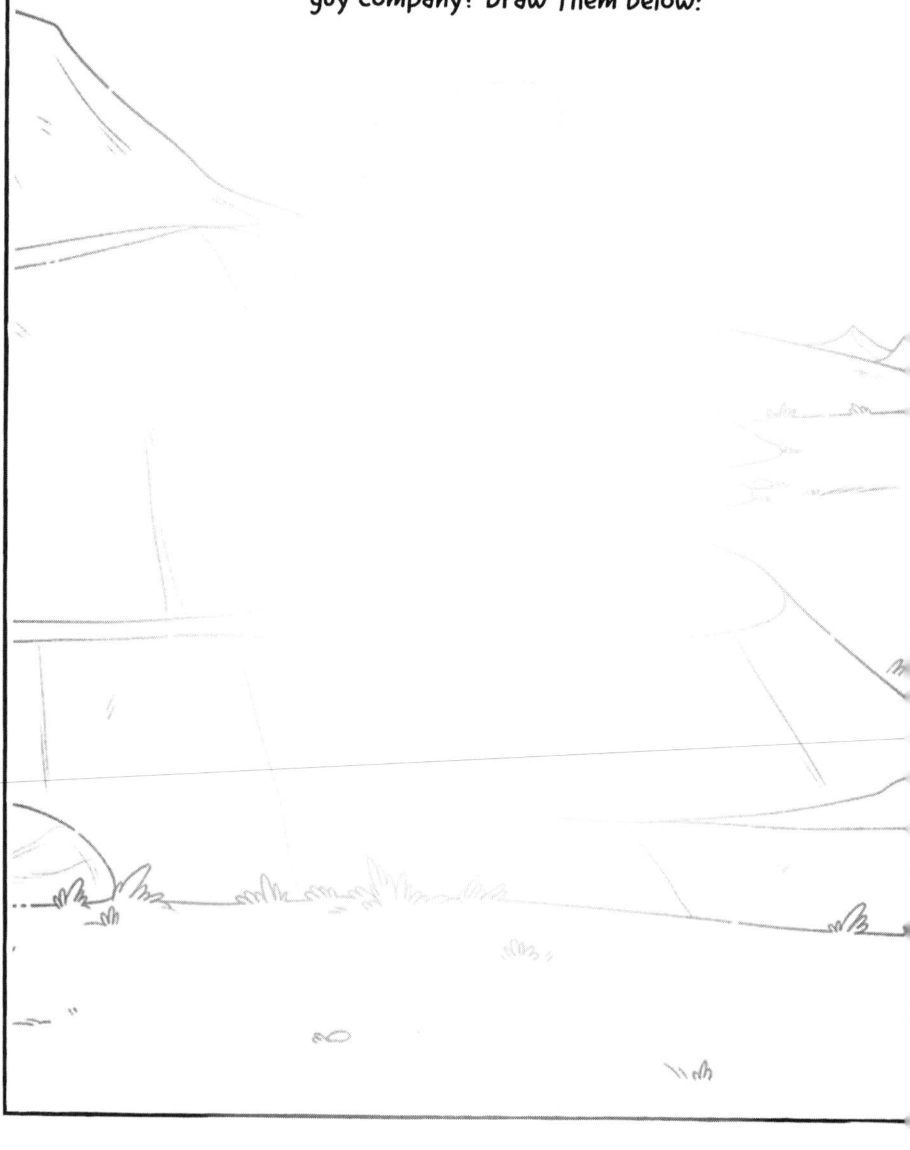

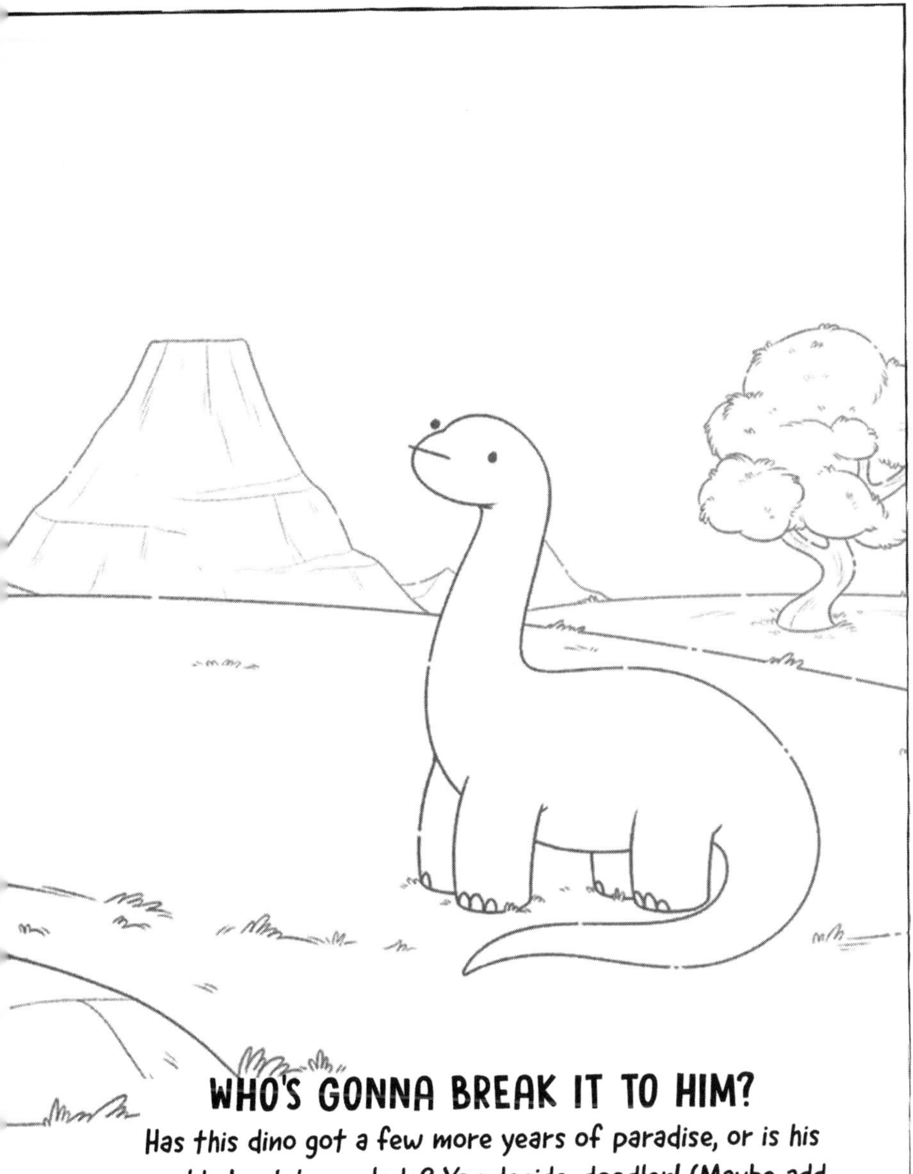

WHO'S GONNA BREAK IT TO HIM?

Has this dino got a few more years of paradise, or is his world about to explode? You decide, doodler! (Maybe add some color to this scene for extra drama!)

WOW! WHAT A COOL . . . PET?

What sort of creature is in the habitat? Draw them.

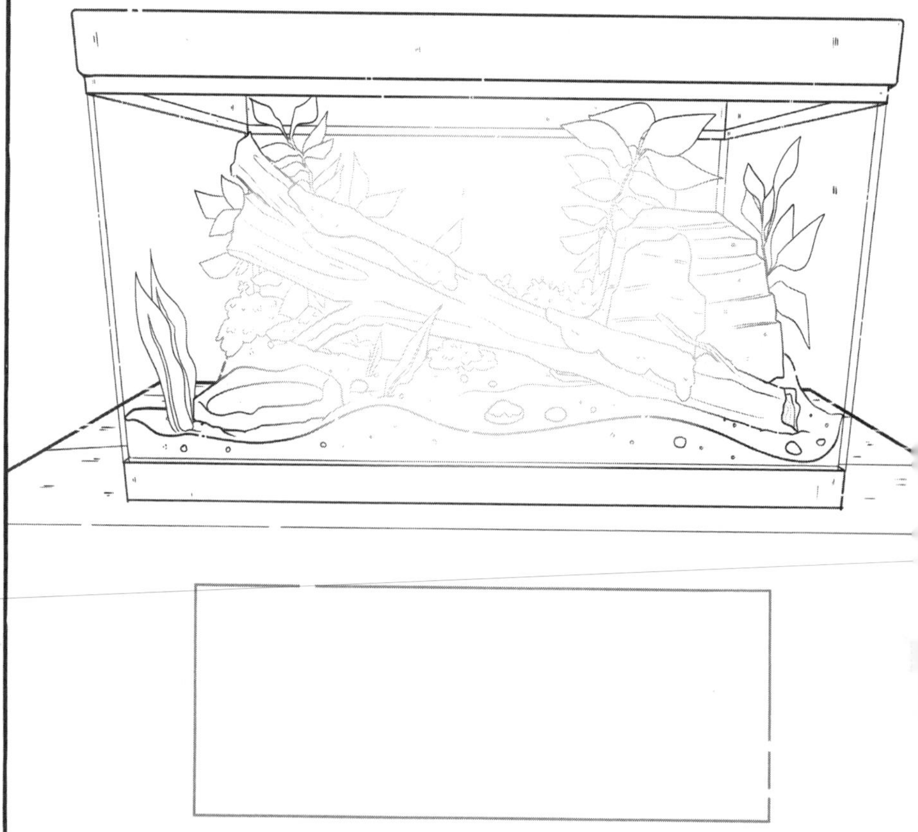

Don't forget to give them a name! Put it on this sign!

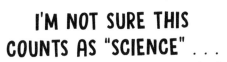

I'M NOT SURE THIS COUNTS AS "SCIENCE"...

Draw this kid's crazy science project.

GROSS!! WHAT'S IN THERE??

James hasn't cleaned out his freezer in . . . a while.
Draw what might be growing.

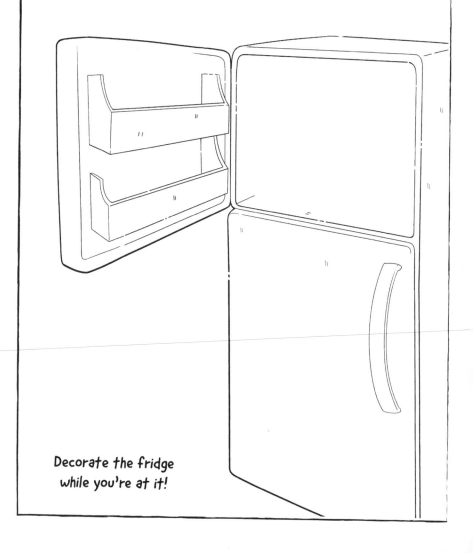

Decorate the fridge
while you're at it!

WE'RE ALL MAD HERE!
Who else is at the mad tea party?

SMILE! YOU'RE ON CAMERA!

James is at an ugly sweater party.
What's James wearing?

YOUR TURN!
What would your ugly sweater
look like, doodler?

WHO'S UP FOR A SNACK?

What kind of treats will James be eating?

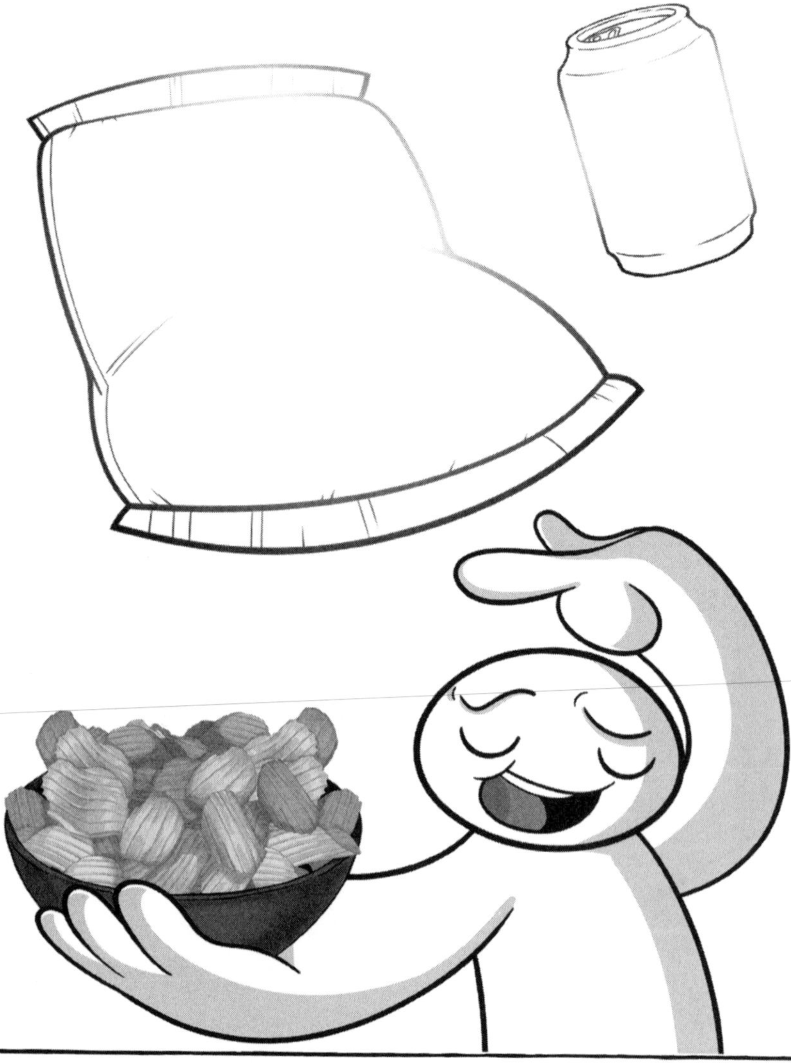

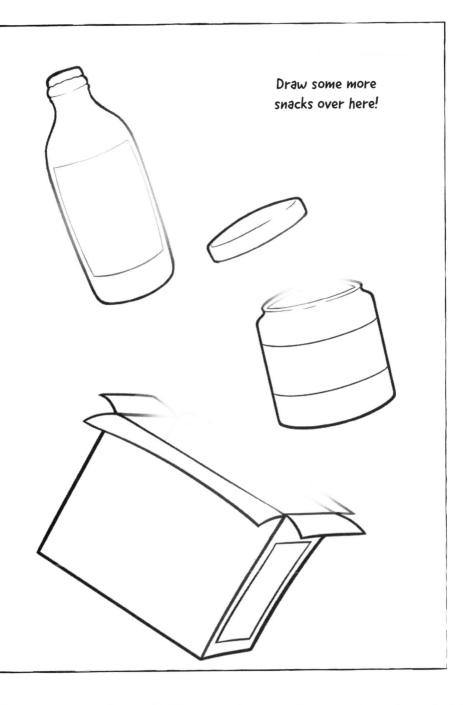

Draw some more
snacks over here!

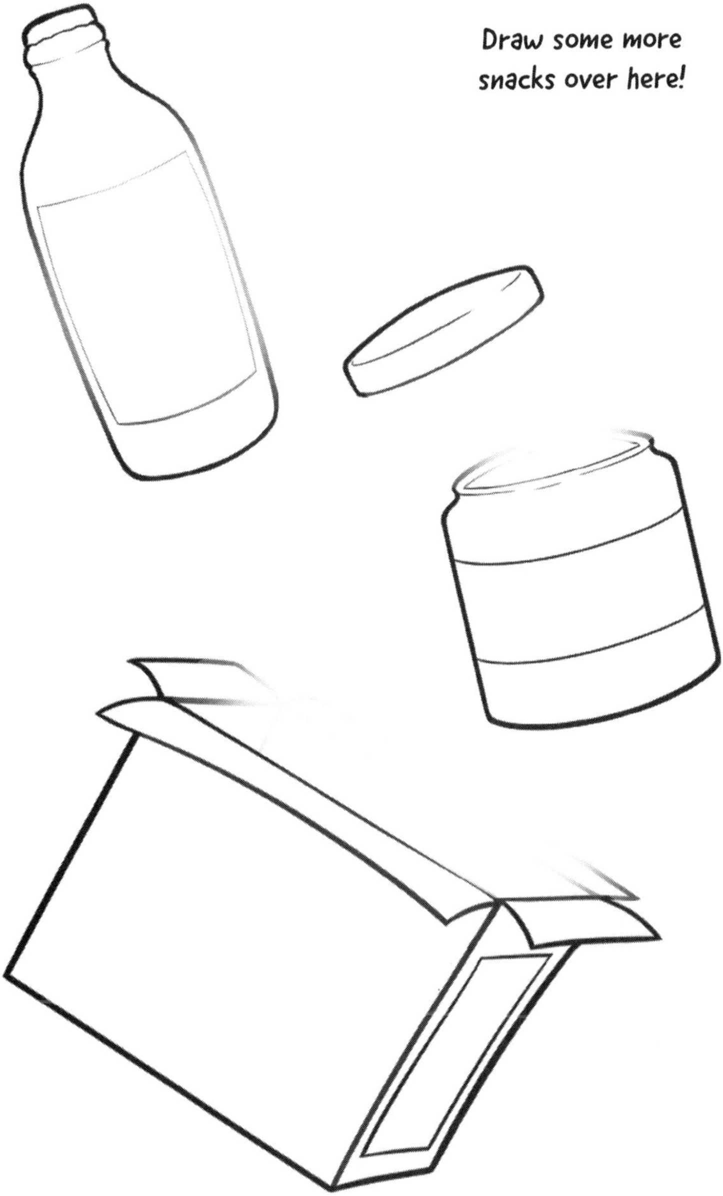

AHHH!! WHAT IS THAT??
Draw what creature has emerged from the forest!

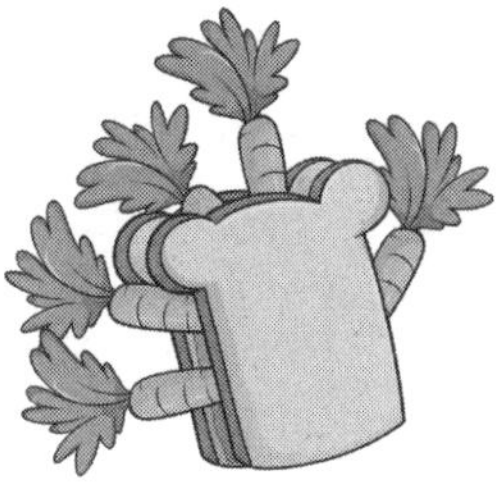

A CARROT SANDWICH??

Gross! You can do better than that!

Draw a delicious sandwich.

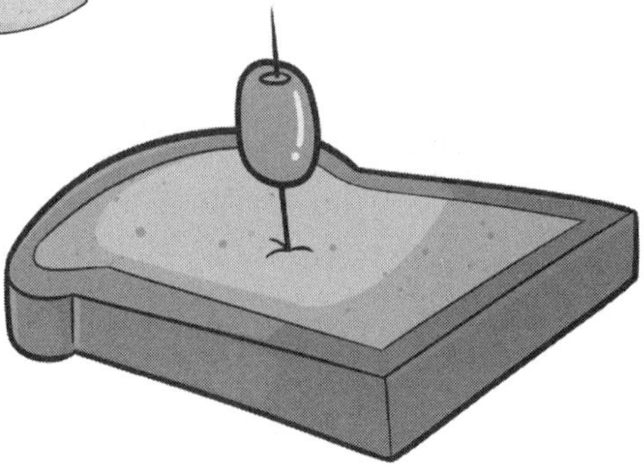

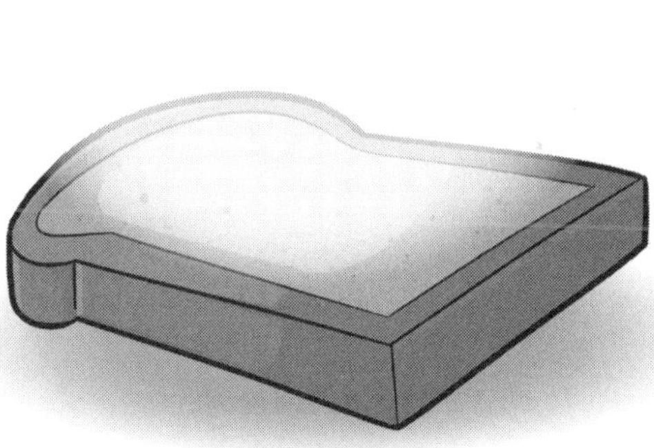

WARPING IN 3 . . . 2 . . . 1!
James is going through some kind of portal!
What dimension is he in right now?

...And where is he going to end up?

ROAD TRIP TIME! WAIT, WHERE'S THE CAR?

Well, you're not going anywhere without a vehicle!
Draw James a sick ride!

Where is James off to?
Draw some scenery!

HAPPY VALENTINE'S DAY!

What did Lizard Cupid put in the Valentine's Day gift?
Draw it below.

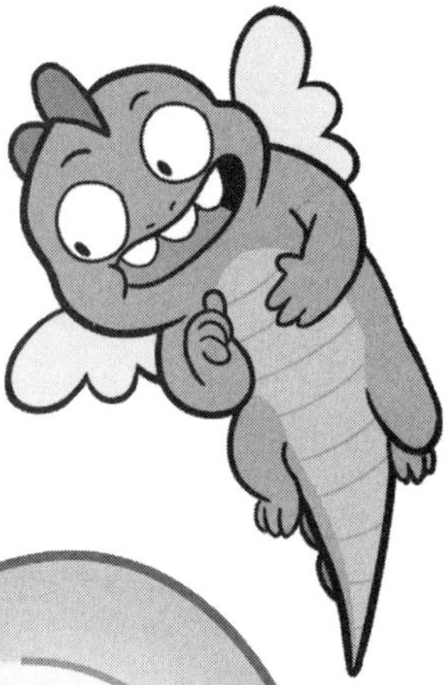

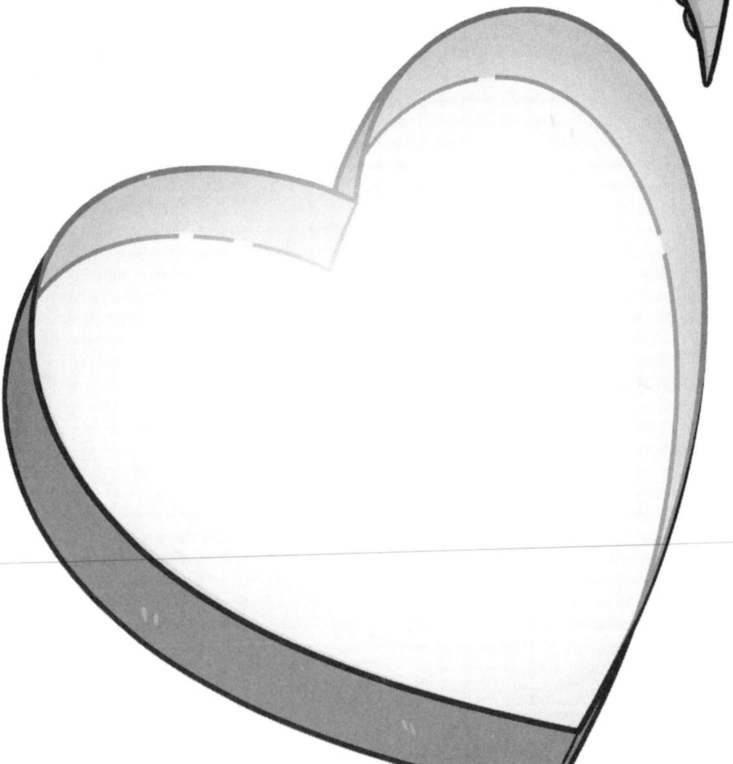

GOODNIGHT!
Sleep tight! What adventure
is Floof having in her dreams?

MEET & GREET

HEY! NICE TO MEET YOU!
Thanks for doodling with me. Do you want a picture?

tárcherperigee

an imprint of Penguin Random House LLC
penguinrandomhouse.com

TarcherPerigee with tp colophon is a registered trademark of
Penguin Random House LLC.

Most TarcherPerigee books are available at special quantity discounts for
bulk purchase for sales promotions, premiums, fund-raising, and educational needs.
Special books or book excerpts also can be created to fit specific needs.
For details, write: SpecialMarkets@penguinrandomhouse.com.

Trade paperback ISBN: 9780593539453

Printed in the United States of America
1st Printing